VISUAL ANALYTICS FOR MANAGEMENT

This book provides students with an in-depth understanding of the concepts, frameworks and processes used to analyze and present visual data for better decision-making. Expert contributors provide guidance in translating complex concepts from large data sets and how this translation drives management practice.

The book's first part provides a descriptive consideration of state-of-the-art science in visual design. The second part complements the first with a rich set of cases and visual examples, illustrating development and best practice to provide students with real-world context. Through their presentation of modern scientific principles, the editors inspire structured discussions of audience and design, recognizing differences in need, bias and effective processes across contexts and stakeholders.

This cutting-edge resource will be of value to students in business analytics, business communication and management science classes, who will learn to be capable managers through the effective and direct visual communication of data. Researchers and practitioners will also find this an engaging and informative book.

Elliot Bendoly is the 2015 Academy of Management's Operations Management Division Distinguished Scholar and a Full Professor in the Fisher College of Business at The Ohio State University, USA.

Sacha Clark is the founder of Mulsanne Management, USA, a firm that assists clients with business strategy development and implementation, productivity enhancement and technology exploitation, and change and transformation management. He has worked with leading companies such as FedEx, General Motors, IBM, Mitsubishi, Procter & Gamble, Pennzoil, Shell, Samsung and WestPac.

In no other source will you find so much helpful knowledge and so many examples of the psychological and decision-making context behind visual representations of data. Serious visual analytics professionals need to be aware of and address these issues if they wish to be effective.

Thomas H. Davenport, *Babson College, USA*

VISUAL ANALYTICS FOR MANAGEMENT

Translational Science and Applications in Practice

Edited by Elliot Bendoly and Sacha Clark

Routledge
Taylor & Francis Group

NEW YORK AND LONDON

First published 2017
by Routledge
711 Third Avenue, New York, NY 10017

and by Routledge
2 Park Square, Milton Park, Abingdon, Oxon OX14 4RN

Routledge is an imprint of the Taylor & Francis Group, an informa business

© 2017 Taylor & Francis

Library of Congress Cataloging in Publication Data
A catalog record for this book has been requested

ISBN: 978-1-138-19071-9 (hbk)
ISBN: 978-1-138-19072-6 (pbk)
ISBN: 978-1-315-64089-1 (ebk)

Typeset in Bembo
by codeMantra

Printed and bound in the United States of America by Sheridan

CONTENTS

FIGURES

TABLES

CONTRIBUTORS

(Listed in Chapter order)

Elliot Bendoly
Fisher College of Business, The Ohio State University

Sacha Clark
Mulsanne Management Ltd

Alice Comi
Department of Management Studies, Aalto University School of Business

Martin Eppler
Institute for Media and Communications Management, University of St. Gallen

L. Alberto Franco
Management Science and Operations Management, Loughborough University

Jukka Huhtamäki
Tampere University of Technology

Martha G. Russell
mediaX, Human Sciences Technology Advanced Research Institute, Stanford University

Kaisa Still
VTT Technical Research Centre of Finland

Jeremy C. Adams
Strategic Planning and Execution at Cardinal Health

Erika Braun
Design Research and Development Graduate Program, The Ohio State University

Sian Joel-Edgar
Computer Science, University of Bath

Lei Shi
Engineering and Design, University of Bath

Lia Emanuel
Computer Science, University of Bath

Simon Jones
Computer Science, University of Bath

Leon Watts
Computer Science, University of Bath

Linda Newnes
Engineering and Design, University of Bath

Stephen Payne
Computer Science, University of Bath

Ben Hicks
Engineering Systems and Design, University of Bristol

Stephen Culley
Engineering and Design, University of Bath

Randi Foraker
Division of Epidemiology, The Ohio State University

James W. Hamister
Raj Soin College of Business, Wright State University

Michael J. Magazine
Carl H. Lindner College of Business, University of Cincinnati

George G. Polak
Raj Soin College of Business, Wright State University

Paul Rosenthal
Department of Computer Science, Technische Universität Chemnitz

Linda Pfeiffer
Department of Computer Science, Technische Universität Chemnitz

Nicholas Hugo Müller
Department of Humanities, Technische Universität Chemnitz

Georg Valtin
Department of Humanities, Technische Universität Chemnitz

David Staley
Department of History, The Ohio State University

Shaun Fontanella
Center for Urban and Regional Analysis, GIS Graduate Program at The Ohio State University

PREFACE

We're drowning in a sea of digital content, data and information. A 2015 study (*Virtualization & Cloud News*, April 5, 2105) determined that every second, the world generates nearly 30 gigabytes (GB) of data—that's enough to fill ten million Blu-ray discs per day. Those discs stacked on top of one another would be as tall as four Eiffel Towers, and that growth rate is accelerating by the moment.

By the same token, technology vendors are also flooding the market with ever more capable, flexible data analytics and visualization tool sets that are becoming more and more accessible and affordable.

That should be good news, but with an abundance of technologies to apply to this tidal wave of content, the bad news is that it's all the more important to address the perennial challenge of *what* data to present to whom and *how* to choose the right representational means.

The challenge of designing the right data and information presentation on an automobile dashboard is a familiar analogy. It helps to illustrate some of the trade-offs inherent in providing professionals and executives with the right dashboard format and content to help them make good decisions. Today's automobile technology is rapidly evolving to the point where drivers already have a palette of choices for custom configuring their individual dashboards (and, in some cases, heads-up displays).

However, is all of that choice necessarily a good thing? Consider the tablet-delivered digital dashboard in Figure R.1—the technology to create this kind of display exists today in the form of cables to connect to vehicles' OBD-II port (on-board diagnostics ports found on every modern vehicle), special software and a tablet. But because data about high-pressure oil pump (HPOP) pressure is available, does that mean that the average driver's attention should be diluted by it? And while the operator of a commercial vehicle or piece of heavy equipment may need to monitor values like engine and transmission oil temperatures, should

FIGURE R.1 Tablet-delivered Digital Dashboard

Source: Macrovector/bigstockphoto

you and I attempt to track that data while navigating the family sedan down the motorway?

Coming from an executive who has spent most of his career engaged in the application of emerging technologies to transform business practices for the better, this may seem almost heretical: I would submit that, for the average driver who is commuting to and fro at normal posted speeds, the vintage car dashboard content and presentation in Figure R.2 is far more effective. It displays an absolute indication of vehicle speed, relative values for engine coolant temperature and fuel levels, and it has warning lamps ("idiot lights") that illuminate in the event of a potentially catastrophic low-oil pressure or improper battery charging condition. As minimalistic as that may be, compared to our first example, it does a far better job of providing the right amount of information to the "average driver." No more than a quick glance allows that driver to get the necessary information for everyday driving conditions while staying focused on the primary task at hand.

Figure R.3, on the other hand, shows a racing car's dashboard. The speeds and competitive environment faced by the racer demands laser-like focus on what's happening on the track and the ability to tune out any and all distractions. At first blush, the plethora of gauges may seem to contradict the earlier points extolling the simplicity of the vintage car's dashboard. However, drivers competing in events that cover long distances at high speed need to monitor a number of indicators of their vehicles' health. Those indicators will directly impact strategy over the course of a multiple-hour race.

The gauges on this car are arranged so that they require little more than using peripheral vision, or, at most, that quick glance. Engine speed is the most important data point and therefore the tachometer is several times larger than all of

FIGURE R.2 Vintage Vehicle Dashboard

Source: BCFC/bigstockphoto

FIGURE R.3 Race Car Dashboard

Source: Barry Blackburn/shutterstock

the other gauges. Also, all of the gauges are oriented in such a way that, when all data values are in their optimal ranges, all of the orange needles are pointed to "12 o'clock"—straight up and down. If something is out of whack, the driver can quickly zero in on the gauge that is showing an abnormal reading and take the appropriate decisions.

In business, it's imperative to sort out the *what*—data and information needs within an enterprise vary as widely as, if not more than, those described in the automotive analogy above. Applying the techniques and concepts from seminal works such as Norton and Kaplan's *The Balanced Scorecard: Translating Strategy into Action* and Huling, Covey and McChesney's *4 Disciplines of Execution: Getting Strategy Done* enables enterprise measurement blueprints that contain well-aligned combinations of leading and lagging indicators. The blueprints define measures and metrics at every level of the organization that ultimately roll up to, and are aligned with, the business's overall strategy.

This book, in turn, provides useful examples of frameworks and implementations that help create the right "gauges" and "warning lights" for individuals in various enterprise roles and levels—the how. The authors illustrate how various strategy-aligned measurement blueprints are transformed into effective presentations of management content, data and information. These insights help create visual business dashboards to keep decision makers informed with the right performance and information read-outs. Well-designed data visualizations ensure that the quick glance tells your "drivers" what they need to know in order to take any necessary actions or decisions.

We hope that you enjoy the book and that it helps you and your stakeholders to stay on track and ahead of the competition.

Sacha Clark
CEO
Mulsanne Management Ltd

INTRODUCTION

Translation. The communication of something's meaning through an equivalent representation. The word derives from the Latin for "a carrying across"—and indeed the gulfs that need to be crossed can sometimes be daunting. The term has a long history of use in the study of languages, with one of the most evocative symbols being that of the famed Rosetta Stone.

When I visited the British Museum with my family in 2013, I couldn't miss this. Seeing it in person, knowing it was the real thing and not a replica, had a visceral effect on me. I had first learned about the Rosetta Stone from Carl Sagan's series COSMOS (Episode 12: Encyclopedia Galactica, 1980). The stone was found by Pierre Bouchard, a French soldier under Napoleon's command during the Egyptian campaign in 1799. It contained portions of passages written in Greek, Egyptian hieroglyphics and Egyptian demotic. By the time of Napoleon however, an understanding of the literal meaning of hieroglyphics and their composite passages, adorning monuments across Egypt, had been lost to time. Egyptologist Jean-Francois Champollion, an expert in languages (including Greek and demotic), ultimately deciphered the hieroglyphics two decades later. To do so he leveraged the fact, or rather the assumption at the time, that the three passages on the stone each had the same meaning.

However the task was not simply one that involved determining which set of hieroglyphic symbols represented which words in Greek or demotic. It required developing an understanding of how these "words" were comprised. Ultimately, Champollion determined that some of the symbols indeed represented sounds (phonetic signs), while others represented entire conceptual meanings in and of themselves (ideographic signs) (Figure I.1).

The choice of the ancient Egyptians to develop a written language that made the simultaneous use of both simple and highly complex signs, although doing the later European scholars no favors, was an artifact of their context and history.

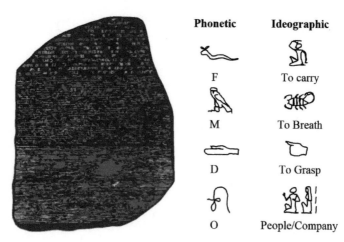

Phonetic	Ideographic
F	To carry
M	To Breath
D	To Grasp
O	People/Company

FIGURE I.1 The Rosetta Stone and Examples of Phonetic and Ideographic Signs

It made sense to be able to succinctly capture commonly confronted concepts in unique images, while allowing for a system of signs to permit the evolution of the written language. It was efficient in some sense, and certainly not the only instance of such an effort by mankind—take for example the Japanese joint use of Kanji ideographs along with Hiragana and Katakana phonetics.

The world is full of simple signs that serve as fundamental building blocks of visual expression. The world is also full of richer signs, not necessarily more complex in terms of the number of pen strokes (or pixels) used to form them, but vastly more sophisticated in the meaning they are intended to express. The trick for the user of these signs is in understanding the audience to which they are attempting to convey meaning. If the audience has a frame of reference equivalent to the communicator, issues of translation aren't raised. However when the audience has a different background, the task needs to be approached in a more sensitive manner. A C-suite manager can be just as stymied by a report developed by modern data analysis as can a French soldier stumbling on pretty pictures carved into a stone.

In this text, we hope to provide a little guidance for those charged with translating complex concepts gleaned from large data sets and sophisticated analysis. The kind of guidance that can facilitate translation and have the greatest chance of driving practice. Our hope is to appeal to both casual readers and dedicated researchers/practitioners critically examining their own processes.

For instructional interests, our book is designed as an accompaniment to primary texts in business analytics coursework as well as to texts in business and technical communications coursework. For those focusing on data analytics as a career path, the ability to leverage data visualization as an analytical approach in parallel to mathematical, statistical and computational modeling in undeniable. For those positioning themselves as capable management communicators, the virtues of effective and direct visual communication of data is similarly without question. As instructors delivering curriculum in support of either of these paths, our hope is that the present text offers much needed support.

More specifically, the assistance needed in both instructional cases goes beyond the simple presentation of stunning infographics and requires structured discussions of audience and problem focus in design; looking not just at end consumer audiences but also at intermediate users of data visualization in analytical development. It requires recognizing differences in need, bias and effective processes across contexts and stakeholders; rationalizing the effectiveness of lean or sophisticated representations; static versus dynamic interactive ones, again with a focus on need; solitary idioms versus dashboard systems of such, as well as how to effectively design these.

To accomplish this and set in place best practices for managers and analysts, it is critical to provide them with well-defined frameworks and processes, based on modern scientific principles and backed with rich case examples of use. This ultimate aim is facilitated by a two-section structure. The first section of this text provides a descriptive consideration of the state-of-the-art and science in visual design. The second provides case examples describing development and/or use in practice, with vivid visual artifacts associated with such work provided as an insert.

It is our sincere hope that all readers find these to be both informative and inspirational in their own work, and that ours will be remembered as only the first of many forays in the intelligent development of visual analytics.

Dr. Elliot Bendoly
Professor of Management Science
Fisher College of Business, The Ohio State University

PART I
The Science of the Art

1

INCOMPLETE PICTURES

Elliot Bendoly

W.E. Deming is quoted as saying "You can expect what you inspect." Not exactly a phrase that roles off the tongue, but an important premise nonetheless. It implies that since most systems can be decomposed into inputs, outputs and connecting processes, intelligence into the details of each of these can facilitate precise mappings of cause–effect relationships; relationships necessary for the anticipation of risks and opportunities, and therefore the discerning of means for improvement. In the absence of complete details, such mappings suffer.

Yet, despite being much more widely (and incorrectly) referenced, Deming never actually suggested "You can't manage what you can't measure." Human decision makers are not incapable of making very good, even optimal, decisions in the absence of complete information. After all that's almost always what we are confronted with, even in the age of "big data." The trick is being able to make use of smart rules, and not falling into traps formed by our own biases.

In this chapter we begin with a description of the boundedly rational mind, drawing on now traditional economic literature on decision theory. We describe the assumptions and implications of this perspective, in practical terms focusing on the manner in which individuals make sense of the world around them. We then extend this discussion by considering three families of biases that specifically affect the way individuals extrapolate from limited data in an effort to make intelligent decisions. Specifically we discuss what we refer to as Set Biases (beliefs in data Homogeneity, Uniformity, Normality), Trend Biases (beliefs in associative data Linearity, Continuity, Unboundedness, Stasis), and Causal Biases (beliefs in relational data Immediacy, No coincidences, Absence of feedback loops). We describe the implications of such biases in the presence of contemporary visual depictions of data; depictions which often do not provide enough details that might otherwise avoid boundedly rational extrapolations and better inform decisions on immediate inspection.

1.1   How We Make Lemonade

As stated, most of the decisions we make are done in the absence of complete information out of practical necessity. Nevertheless humans have survived as a species so far, so we must be doing something right. It turns out, when handed the lemon-equivalent of data, humans have a remarkable knack for making lemonade; and more often than not it tastes pretty good.

How do we do it? What is this talent?

In large part we benefit from our ability to construct and reference rules for making sense of our environment. This is a skill developed over the eons of the evolution of our species. Those that maintained efficient and effective rule sets could scan their environment for risks and opportunities, formulate tactics for evading or leveraging, and out-perform those who held less efficient or less effective rules. From a translational perspective, it was as if the high performers had Google Maps advising them on how to plan their routes, while the low performers only had an aerial photograph; i.e. the difference in large part was in how the data available was converted to actionable compositions.

Today we often discuss the process by which we transform data that we observe into potential action as "sensemaking." Sensemaking as a concept is something we'll talk about a lot in this text, as it is not simply an inherent ability that individuals possess but also an ability that can be developed. It is also something that is key in the development of artificial intelligence. Granted, sometimes that development is in the wrong direction; individuals or artificial agents latch on to a new rule based on erroneous observation. But in other instances it can lead to much more intelligent decision making, in some cases superseding older less effective rules. And thankfully, course corrections in development are also always possible, albeit at some cost.

Whether correct or not, these rules that we construct include beliefs regarding simple associations as well as complex causal relationships. These are mental maps that draw connections between observations and outcomes desired, peppered with details regarding the constraints within which these nodes and connections exist. They also include details regarding the lags between action and response, though as humans we do have some difficulty remembering to account for these at times.

We also tend to hold more than one line of reasoning, more than one mental map, in our arsenals. After all, we are social creatures. We encounter others who have different views of causality, and no matter how much we might like to we never completely ignore these views. That of course does complicate how we make sense of our environment. Ultimately our choices of rule sets to go with rely on higher-level meta-rules. Metaheuristics, and at the highest level something that would seem so basic but has long been far too ignored in management: preference.

There are other words you'll encounter when discussing decision making with scholars. The rules that define how inputs are converted into decisions often fall into the category of "heuristics," with metaheuristics again referring to those higher-level rules that help develop and select which heuristic best applies to

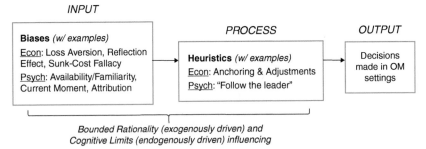

FIGURE 1.1 An Input–Process–Output View of Sensemaking (pro tem. omitting feedback)

a certain scenario. The term "bias" also tends to come up, although any quick examination of extant sources (including the more credible corners of Wikipedia) will reveal a good deal of blurring between what falls into the classification of bias versus heuristics. For the purpose of a concrete discussion, let's borrow a page again from the Operations Management field and think about sensemaking from an input–process–output (IPO) perspective.

As shown in Figure 1.1, heuristics and metaheuristics are nicely positioned as processes by which inputs are converted into decisions. What are inputs then? Certainly the observations we are able to make or data are by other means provided regarding the context of the decision. However inputs also include personal tendencies to give more weight to certain kinds of data than to others. The biases are the adjectives to the nouns that comprise our decision-making environments, and often serve as adverbs to color the heuristics we apply in decision making. Some examples of these biases, drawn from the elder disciplines of Economics and Psychology are provided in Figure 1.1. Although it isn't the intent of this text to provide a comprehensive examination of biases and heuristics suggested by researchers, it benefits our present discussion to go through just some of these.

1.2 Biases in Everyday Life

To be sure, biases and heuristics are not all bad. They have a history of being absolutely critical to decision making; without them many great decisions may never have been made in the timely fashion in which they were needed. But it should also be clear that their presence, persistence and acceptance is not without some very relevant risks. Sometimes the lemonade we make gives us an ulcer. It can even be lethal, and sadly not only to the decision maker.

On the input side, focusing on the various ways inherent biases might be influencing us, we'll start our review with a big one. A bias that is embedded in many, if not most data interpretations and selections of/mediations of decision processes people face on a daily basis: Loss Aversion.

Loss Aversion

The tendency for individuals to strongly prefer (a) avoiding losses versus (b) acquiring gains. Made famous by Kahneman and Tversky (1981, 1984), and their investigation of the Allais Paradox, this bias has been studied extensively. The initial observations of this bias involved examining the following question posed to physicians:

> The U.S. is preparing for the outbreak of an unusual Asian disease, which is expected to kill 600 people. Two alternative programs to combat the disease have been proposed. Assume that the exact scientific estimates of the consequences of the programs are as follows: If program A is adopted, 200 people will be saved. If program B is adopted, there is a one-third probability that 600 people will be saved and a two-thirds probability that no people will be saved. Which of the two programs would you favor?

72 percent of those asked chose option A, the certainty of 200 survivals over the possibility of 600 deaths. Interestingly the same options were provided in a somewhat different wording to examine how phrasing alone might impact choice:

> The U.S. is preparing for the outbreak of an unusual Asian disease, which is expected to kill 600 people. Two alternative programs to combat the disease have been proposed. Assume that the exact scientific estimates of the consequences of the programs are as follows: If program C is adopted, 400 people will die. If program D is adopted, there is a one-third probability that nobody will die and a two-thirds probability that 600 people will die. Which of the two programs would you favor?

To their surprise only 22 percent selected option C (equivalent in lives saved to option A), with 78 percent preferring option D (exact wording as B). A dramatic swing in what one might view as apparent "preference." The swing captures what is referred to as the Reflection Effect—the tendency for the preferences of individuals in Loss (or Loss framed) scenarios to appear to be the mirror opposite of those apparent in Gain (or Gain framed) scenarios.

A somewhat more striking comparison is the consideration of the following two choice scenarios. In one, the choice is one between a certain gain of $20 or a one-third chance of gaining $60. In the other the choice is between a certain loss of $20 and a one-third chance of losing $60. Two equal gains in one case, two equal losses in the other. Studies demonstrate a strong preference for certain gains in the first case, but a strong preference for uncertain losses in the other.

Again, a swing in preference?

Not technically, and this is something that scholars often get wrong. The fundamental nature of "preference" (the individual bias against loss) wasn't swinging at all—people prefer to avoid loss. That's what they were doing in both cases. What was different was the "perception" of the presence of loss. The salience of loss. In the second case, the perception of loss was amplified by explicit wording to that effect. That is the power of framing, and something that applies both to words and visual images.

This is also not an isolated contextual finding. De Martino et al. (2006) in an article in *Science* describe their more recent observations of this bias through an experiment in which individuals are asked to make choices in one setting for which certain options are described, or "framed," as losses, and another in which certain options are framed as gains. The two settings are detailed in Table 1.1 along with the associated percent of participants choosing each option.

Note specifically that the first choice in both settings is to walk away with $30 (leave behind $20) of the $50 originally given. However, simply framing this as a loss is enough to shift participants towards a more risky option, and one with a lower expected value of $25. Findings like these emphasize the power of Loss Aversion as it impacts the choices we make. If the rule, or heuristic, or verb in the decision process is "select the option that lets you experience the most gain," Loss Aversion serves to color those possible gains (or color their respective losses). It changes the perception of things. Through these perceptions it influences the manner in which an otherwise sound heuristic might play out.

While Loss Aversion focuses on the perception of prospective losses and gains simply by virtue of the loss orientation or loss framing of choices, other related biases can also impact these perceptions. Some emerge from past experience, as in the case of the Sunk-Cost Fallacy.

Sunk-Cost Fallacy

The belief that additional investment in an option is needed based on past invest-ment, often with the associated belief that such past investments would otherwise be lost and despite the potential risk of loss from further investment. The past investments in this case are unrecoverable expenditures of money, time, capital, etc. In other words what are referred to as sunk costs. The "fallacy" here is that individuals tend to disproportionately weigh the value of options for which unre-coverable past investments (sunk costs) have been made, relative to new options all other things being equal. In many cases individuals chose options that are explicitly less favorable because of past investments. In experiments, much like the emphasis of loss, an emphasis on prior investments in an option has been shown

TABLE 1.1 Results of a Loss Framing Experiment

	Setting 1 – Start with $50		Setting 2 – Start with $50	
Choices	Keep $30	50/50 chance of keeping or losing $50	Lose $20	50/50 chance of keeping or losing $50
% Who Chose	57%	43%	39%	61%

to greatly influence choice—again coloring perception and allowing otherwise effective choice heuristics to go awry.

How might that impact the views of individuals well versed in the construction of visual data representations of one sort when asked to expand their analysis? Are they more likely to start from scratch with a potentially new and valuable perspective, or invest further in simply tweaking artifacts they have spent time developing?

There have been some recent counter arguments regarding whether a bias towards options with greater sunk costs is in fact "irrational." Some have suggested that further commitment to such options fulfills a social–psychological need: specifically to demonstrate to others that you knew what you were doing all along (if success is gained) or to demonstrate simply that you are unwavering in your commitments. These additional factors of course change the actual value of the option, with the potential to make it more favorable in real terms relative to other options not yet invested in. In other words, this doesn't prevent individuals from still disproportionately weighing options with sunk costs… it just makes such overweighing irrelevant. In such cases the "all other things being equal" no longer applies.

It's easy to have the presence and influence of biases masked by other details. That doesn't mean they are not present or influential. Indeed it is not uncommon for both the Sunk-Cost Fallacy and Loss Aversion to simultaneously impact the perceived value of choices. Consider the two additional related biases of Availability and Current Moment.

Availability Bias

Individuals tend to overly weigh the value of options that they are able to recall the most detail. As a result, those options of which individuals have the most recent or most extensive experience and familiarity are favored, all other things being equal, to options for which less familiarity exists. This aspect of the Availability Bias has led to a common reference to what scholars refer to as the Familiarity Bias.

Current Moment Bias

Often referred to by the term Hyperbolic Discounting, the Current Moment Bias is the tendency for individuals to overweigh more near-term payoffs relative to payoffs available later (Laibson 1997).

While these biases can stand alone in their own right, it is clear that there are many instances in which these also will have a dual presence. The details of the near-term are typically clearer than the details of the long-term. It's not uncommon, therefore, for current payoffs to appeal not only because they seem more readily available, but also because the amount of information available about these (their familiarity) is often greater. Still more confounding, past investments (sunk cost) in certain options can often provide familiarity with such options. Many options are also positioned to yield short-term gains, albeit at long-term expense. It is no surprise that much of commercial marketing emphasizes familiarity and near-term benefit, while pitching costs as existing substantially further in the future and de-emphasizing what such costs entail.

The only real question is why society as a whole remains boggled by the systematic nature and permanency of debt.

1.3 Biases in the Perception of Data

The biases just discussed have been discussed generally in reference to the facts presented when individuals are faced with isolated decisions. In other words the "data" that they are often thought to be coloring is typically very limited. The value of a lottery ticket. The number of individuals surviving an epidemic. The lowest cost option for obtaining a vehicle. But biases also apply to assumptions made about collectives, groups of things. Consider for example the various biases that have been identified by social psychologists in the study of behavior in group settings. Case in point is the Group Attribution Error, or the bias towards imagining that one or a subset of entities is characteristic of the larger set as a whole; a bias that can stubbornly remain even in light of new information to the contrary. Because individuals are making generalizations regarding the attributes of and within groups of people, places or things, we refer to biases such as this as intrascopic—with the prefix "intra" emphasizing the biases' implications on how the internal nature of collections is perceived.

Similar intrascopic biases also play a particularly important role in our perception of more complex forms of data. Distributions that have more than "a dot"; histories and cross-sections of data collected across multiple populations; data where multiple mechanisms comprising distinct forms of risks and paths for evolution may exist. To understand why it is important to think about more than monolithic views of biases, it is critical to appreciate how we approach non-monolithic data and in particular what we risk losing when we don't have all the dots we need. For discussion purposes we will group these biases as they relate to aspects of descriptive, predictive and prescriptive analysis.

Set Biases

In the process of examining data, individuals tend to make a number of assumptions right off the bat. The most common of these includes the assumption of homogeneity across samples. This implies a singular constituency, and subsequently often leads to difficulty in accounting for the noise in data; occasionally leading to misdirected conclusions. Simpson's Paradox (or Amalgamation Paradox) as depicted in Figure 1.2 is a nice example of how easily the homogeneity

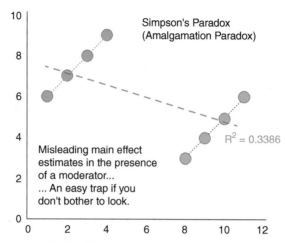

FIGURE 1.2 Homogeneity Set Biases as Represented by Simpson's Paradox

Set Bias can wreak havoc with analysis. In this Paradox, best fits to subsets of data suggest trends diametrically contrary to those that would be estimated if the subsets were not distinguished.

Another common bias is the belief that the distribution of the data set adheres to a common symmetrical form (e.g. uniform and normal being the most common, largely due to how students are first introduced to distributions in basic statistics). This symmetry Set Bias can be more easily checked against by modern statistical methods, and it often does not critically impact analysis—in the case of bimodal distributions, subset distinction can even be resolved. Unfortunately, often these checks are not made prior to model estimation, and in some instances these Set Biases can prove problematic as well.

In contrast it is also clearly possible to imagine instances where populations are not neatly captured by samples, particularly in the case of small samples. In such cases individuals examining data may perceive of clusters that that don't actually exist. Such a phenomena has been referred to as the Clustering Illusion (Iverson et al. 2008). It has also been applied to explain how individuals develop perceptions of how data outside of observable samples might be interpolated or extrapolated. This bring us to our second general category of data biases.

Trend Biases

The Clustering Illusion just described has been associated with the tendency of individuals to excessively focus on small runs or streaks in data observed, and subsequently extrapolating or interpolating based on such limited information. The reason why this is problematic lays in the tendencies by which such extrapolation takes place. Once again largely an artifact of the way individuals have been taught, two major but fundamental assumptions are typically made: (1) that trends

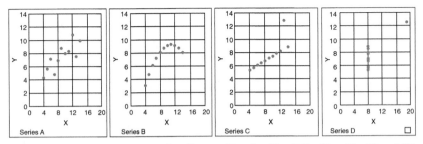

FIGURE 1.3 Anscomb's Quartet (for all sets, $\mu X = 9$, $\mu Y = 7.5$, $\sigma X = 10$, $\sigma Y = 3.75$; linear model estimates: $Y = 0.5X + 3$, $R2 = 0.67$)

are linear, (2) that trends are continuous. These Trend Biases (linearity and continuity) are outcomes of other fundamental biases, such as the belief that over the relevant range trends are unbounded. Interestingly, once individuals question these more fundamental behaviors they are less likely to fall into linearity and continuity bias traps.

Are there additional situational reasons why some individuals default to linear assumptions? Certainly. When individuals personally benefit from conclusions drawn from linearity assumptions, they will tend to make such assumptions (Self-serving Bias). If linearity is what they have always experienced in a data set for which they make decisions, there will also be a tendency for new data, even if seemingly deviating from linearity, to be under weighed or ignored. This is related to the Semmelweis reflex (the tendency to ignore contrary evidence) and the Status Quo Bias from psychology.

The other interesting thing about Trend Biases is that individuals strongly influenced by one are also often influenced by others. There are often broader mindsets, mental models of how data behaves and what to expect of it, which have higher-level influences on the maintenance of biases. A metabias towards linear-continuity for example may be more common than isolated intrascopic biases towards either linearity or continuity.

As an example, consider the following observation. In past talks and classes we often presented audiences with the classic Anscomb's Quartet data sets, as shown in Figure 1.3. The neat bit about each of these four data sets is that their basic descriptive statistics (means and variances for X and Y) are all the same. As are the best fit parameters of a linear fit of Y as a function of X.

Of course we don't tell the audience that before we show the set. Rather we ask them to draw what they feel the "true relationship" between X and Y is. Most people draw straight continuous lines, in some cases simply filtering out points that don't adhere to that line. Some draw curves in particular instances (especially for the second panel's data set as one might expect). A handful draw discontinuous lines.

Figure 1.4 summarizes the typical distribution of results we get from audiences, regardless of background. The responses for depictions in the last panel are

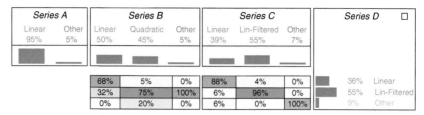

FIGURE 1.4 Responses from Practitioners When Asked to Draw Relationships between X and Y in Each Series

crossed with other responses to emphasize how metabiases can playout in guiding intrascopic Trend Biases. Specifically, around 55 percent of respondents tend to filter out the seeming outliers from the last two panels, and draw best fit non-curved lines running through the rest of the points in these panels.

These are not simply random choices being made. Almost all of those who filter in one case will filter in the other (96 percent). Even more strikingly, 75 percent of those who draw quadratic forms in the second panel will tend to filter in the third and fourth. Sixty-eight percent of those who draw straight lines in the second panel draw straight lines without filtering in the fourth panel. Why? Assumptions of linearity and assumptions regarding the need to filter otherwise discontinuous data. These two can be discussed fairly distinctly. Certainly it is possible for one to exist but not the other (as we have seen). The reason why they tend to be observed together has more to do with the willingness of individuals to entertain the potential complexity of data over their bias towards more simplistic albeit potentially facile views of the world. Something we will discuss in additional depth in the next chapter.

Causal Biases

Whereas intrascopic Trend Biases describe assumptions regarding the form of associations, and thus influence predictive analytics, formalized decision making assisted by prescriptive analysis typically presumes the development of mental models of cause and effect. In other words, not only does one presume "X and Y increase together," but moreover "increasing X forces increases in Y." The difference is between taking a stance as a passive anticipator of dynamics and being poised for the active management of those dynamics. Both Set and Trend Biases can influence the structure of these mental models, however other uniquely Causal Biases may also prove strongly influential in how we form beliefs of cause and effect.

Returning again to the concept of attribution, the Fundamental Attribution Error suggests individuals tend to assign more credit to individual actors and their personalities than to the other situational factors, which are often out of the control of such actors. If this bias is active it clearly can have a significant impact on perspectives of causality in data observed. Data specific to human actors may tend to be viewed as causal to outcomes more often than simply as associative. This can lead not only to poor decision making, but also to undue social stressors that further undermine the effectiveness of processes—not to mention difficult to resolve.

However, attributions of causality do not need to be restricted to the humans involved in the data. As humans we're hard wired to see causality in observations all around us, even when it doesn't exist. This "non-coincidence" metabias drives us to attribute a wide range of human and non-human factors with the capability of driving outcomes. Often erroneously.

What makes certain elements more likely to be attributed as causes of outcomes? The Availability and Current Moment Biases certainly offer some suggestions. Generally speaking, humans are also extremely susceptible to the intrascopic Causal Bias of immediacy—that outcomes immediately follow actions that drive them. This tends to limit our search for likely suspects to actions and agents present at or just prior to the outcome's observation. Obviously that can be a problem, since two events that take place close to each other in time might be separate outcomes of a third factor and otherwise unrelated. When we find nothing proximal to the outcome, we may also concede to a relative lack of control over it. Neither of these suppositions are necessary, provided we are willing to look back far enough and carefully at the systems in which outcomes arise.

Related is the Causal Bias of non-feedback—specifically that an action/agent impacting an outcome will not result in counter-effects that will force subsequent changes in that action/agent. In reality, feedback loops are all around us. They have been widely studied and shown to be critical in the studies of systems. We even create social and legal structures that enforce reciprocity. Yet when faced with decision making, when confronted with visual representations of data that we are unfamiliar with, we have a tendency to overlook the existence of these loops. It implies a bit of egotism regarding the control one has over the decision environment. It also often happens hand in hand with the immediacy bias—if you are only looking for temporally proximal causes, you're also unlikely to recognize feedback mechanisms that take time to play out.

1.4 Heuristics, Metaheuristics and Sensemaking

What ultimately are the implications of all these biases? Specifically, how might they influence the interpretation of contemporary visual depictions of data? Depictions that often do not provide enough details that might otherwise avoid boundedly rational extrapolations and better inform decisions on immediate inspection.

How might/should they influence the design of visual artifacts?

Universally, the ethical design of visual representations of data should be focused on truth and clarity for the audiences targeted. This means not selectively excluding or emphasizing certain aspects contrary to the intent of the conveyance. It also means being deliberate in providing clarity that dodges the kind of erroneous interpretations that common Set, Trend and Causal Biases can drive. Design still benefits from having an organized structure focusing on one or more key messages or with a subset of typical exploration paths in mind. However, these should be developed with transparency. The possibility of counter interpretations should not be constrained deliberately by visual designs, only by the nature of the underlying data (if at all).

Assuming truthfulness is a foremost concern, the question becomes one of how to ensure clarity. As designers, our ability to be clear requires that we both guard against our own possible biases and anticipate those for whom we design. This anticipation requires an appreciation not only of the possibility of biases already mentioned but also of the processes (heuristics) individuals use in the formation of the models; the processes that these biases color.

Not all of these processes are straightforward. Not all of them are easily explained. Most are short cuts, not comprehensive. But that doesn't mean they don't work in a lot of cases. It just means understanding them will help us design things to help make them work better (or even correct for them).

Consider the Nearest-Next heuristic individuals often use when asked to manually solve routing problem (e.g. travelling salesman scenarios as discussed in Bendoly 2013). By this process individuals start with a single element such as location in a route, and select each subsequent element based on closest proximity. It turns out that for highly complex routes, for which a comprehensive search for cost minimizing options increases factorally as a function of sites (N! solutions for a N-site routing problem), this simple process of coming up with a solution will tend to do fairly well—often missing the true optimal path, but also often appearing in the top 10 percent of performing solutions. It's fast and frugal—effective. If we want people to capitalize on such a heuristic in a data representation, we would benefit from the clear presentation of all sites, and a simple visual means by which to connect these dots. If we want our audience to avoid this, if we believe it to be problematic in the specific context, we need to design interfaces that make other interpretations and decision processes easy to conduct.

Another common heuristic is that of Anchoring and Adjustment. The use of this heuristic is often cited in decision-making settings where data continues to be revealed over time. But studies also show that individuals tend to be poor at selecting anchors in certain circumstances, and often insufficiently adjust. The Bayesian concept of Conservatism suggests that many have an inherent tendency to not adjust as much as we often should when presented with new data. If this is a concern, again we need to design data representations that emphasize the importance of new data and perhaps offer intelligent recommendations on how best to anchor.

A seemingly simpler heuristic, at least one that doesn't involve a great deal of processing, is sometimes referred to colloquially as "Follow the leader." Essentially it entails accepting interpretations and decision patterns from other sources, human or automated. Goddard et al. (2011) provide a fascinating study of how individuals can very easily adopt without question the guidance of automated systems, regardless of effectiveness. We do tend to put a great deal of faith in automated systems, rightly so in many cases. We are just as ready to assign blame to these other sources, which to some extent makes "Follow the leader" and associated phenomena such as Group Think to be more a coping mechanisms than anything else. However blind attribution of accuracy and optimality to other sources can be a problem; coping with difficult interpretations and decisions by depending on others is generally not in the best interest of analysis. As designers we need to be careful about how much we automate for our users—when we want to promote active management, allowing them to be strictly passive undermines this goal.

How can we encourage active use? By helping individuals appreciate the systematic nature of the data they are confronted with. By emphasizing its dynamic nature. By emphasizing how data can be viewed as not only associated but potentially causally linked to other data. In the visual representation of data, effective interpretation of such dynamics is strongly facilitated by explicitly denoting direction and feedback, and allowing explorations of incremental changes.

This bring us to a mantra we will continue to reiterate:

System visualizations require systems of visuals.

That is, when there is a need to convey the nature of a complex system of inputs and processes that generate outputs of interest, a single visual idiom is unlikely to be sufficient. Here we conservatively adopt Haber and McNabb's classic definition of a visualization idiom: "any specific sequence of data enrichment and enhancement transformations, visualization mappings, and rendering transformations that produce an abstract display of a specific data set" (1990). Singular idioms, conservatively speaking, are self-contained renderings and tend to be limited, rationally, by a constrained selection of data and choice in abstraction. Because of this any stand-alone rendering will tend to, in isolation, pose a risk of inappropriate interpolations and erroneous extrapolations. In short it can lead to ineffective mental models of cause and effect, and subsequently to suboptimal, potentially disastrous decision making.

What is the alternative to a single visual depiction of a complex system? The answer might seem obvious, but in fact is a bit nuanced. In the case of truly complex systems, the best means of conveying critical dynamics is in fact not providing a comprehensive compilation of all possible system scenarios depicted in a multidimensional space. Just as overwhelming an audience with a talk that provides too many details can lose a message, overwhelming an audience with endless depictions can fail to deliver. As we shall see in the next section there are some good reasons why, returning us again to a consideration of human cognitive constraints. Ultimately the best solutions to complex conveyance require sufficiency as well as selectivity in the design; the construction of efficient systems within which stand-alone idioms can be selectively considered and reconsidered in turn towards the development of sufficient system-wide understanding.

References

Bendoly, E. (2013) *Excel Basics to Blackbelt: An Accelerated Guide to Decision Support Designs* 2nd Edition, New York, NY: Cambridge University Press.

De Martino, B., D. Kumaran, B. Seymour and R.J. Dolan (2006) "Frames, Biases, and Rational Decision-Making in the Human Brain," *Science* 313(5787): 684–687.

Goddard, K., A. Roudsari and J.C. Wyatt (2011) "Automation Bias—A Hidden Issue for Clinical Decision Support System Use," *International Perspectives in Health Informatics. Studies in Health Technology and Informatics* 164: 17–22.

Haber, R.B. and D.A. McNabb (1990) "Visualization Idioms: A Conceptual Model for Scientific Visualization Systems," in *Visualization in Scientific Computing*, G.M. Nielson, B. Shriver and L.J. Rosenblum (eds), Washington: IEEE Computer Society Press.

Iverson, G., B.L. Brooks and J.A. Holdnack (2008) "Misdiagnosis of Cognitive Impairment in Forensic Neuropsychology," In *Neuropsychology in the Courtroom: Expert Analysis of Reports and Testimony*, R.L. Heilbronner, New York, NY: Guilford Press, p. 248.

Kahneman, D. and A. Tversky (1984) "Choices, Values, and Frames," *American Psychologist* 39(4): 341–350.

Laibson, D (1997) "Golden Eggs and Hyperbolic Discounting," *Quarterly Journal of Economics* 112(2): 443–477.

Tversky, A. and D. Kahneman (1981) "The Framing of Decisions and the Psychology of Choice," *Science* 211: 453–458.

2

COPING WITH HAYSTACKS

Elliot Bendoly

In contrast to the first chapter, we devote our discussion here to the pitfalls of information overloads in visual depictions. In doing so we focus on another very real aspect of the human condition: cognitive limits.

Let's start with a curious anecdote.

At the start of 2015, as we were ramping up for our university-wide data visualization competition, a colleague came to talk of his personal views on human cognition. The discussion began unassumingly. We were in strong agreement regarding many points recognized in psychological, communication and design theory. Our colleague clearly had a strong appreciation of the problems that insufficient data representation might create, as well as the roles that biases and heuristics leveraged by designers and audiences can play; points discussed in Chapter 1.

And then he voiced something that immediately took us back. He expressed his belief that there was no such thing as too much information when it came to visual depictions. He dismissed wholesale the notion that individuals might have difficulty meaningfully focusing, filtering or aggregating increasingly complex presentations. His argument: The rule of $7+/-2$ (the so-called Miller's Law) didn't hold water in most of the successful visual representations he and others had experience with. Specifically, since one could come up with countless highly effective examples in which many more than just seven pieces of information are simultaneously graphically and meaningfully displayed—considerations of cognitive limits were largely irrelevant to design.

Our colleague was fairly adamant, despite our suggestion that he might want to reread Tufte's commentary on the subject. He seemed surprised to hear others might not share his fairly cut and dry perspective. I almost felt like hugging the guy.

It can be difficult to separate the robustness of general concepts from the applicability of their specific operationalizations; the forms they are given for tangible albeit specific discussion purposes. This is where our colleague faltered. Miller's Law (not self-named) outlines a very specific numerical instance that was applied to a very specific case context. Miller never suggested the 7+/−2 rule to be literally applicable regardless of context. He intended it to be an exemplar of the broader recognition of human cognitive limitations; limitations that take many forms. Just as no researcher worth her salt would presume a mean or median to be a holistic representation of a distribution (let alone a stable measure of a population or other samples of that population), it is clear that harping about a universally relevant count of anything would be misguided.

We agreed, it's ridiculous to expect any predefined specific number of "things" would represent a limit on visual design. However, that doesn't mean that limits in general are absent in cognition as it relates to visual design and interpretation. Certainly Miller's point, and later related discussions by Tufte, emphasize that throwing this figurative baby out with the literal bath water is in short gross neglect. Of course cognitive limits exist, we just can't easily assign a single number to universally encapsulate them.

How do these limits show themselves in data visualization contexts? Often they emerge when there is so much content confronting us that the boundaries between relevant and irrelevant data, spurious and real relationships, are blurred. It's one of the downsides of data wealth. The more elements you have in a depiction the more likely these blurry lines will show up somewhere. When we push ourselves to show more than is necessary, we often introduce things that distract from interpretation simply because their presence can make it that much harder to focus. It leaves a door open for novel interpretations, but also at extremes it raises the risk that messages are overlooked, that meaningful deduction is frozen. At these extremes, not defined by any one number, ambiguity can shut things down if not completely mislead.

Those in the field of visual design have a similar view. Designers often cite the Law of Prägnanz, another principle based in psychology, which states that individuals have a tendency to interpret ambiguous images as simple and complete, versus complex and incomplete. Notice both the terms "simple" and "complete." In other words, when presentations of data are incomplete, individuals tend to complete these pictures in simple ways—enter the data set, Trend and Causality Biases discussed in Chapter 1. However when data presentations are excessively complex, individuals lacking the cognitive resources to easily process such information are either forced to or choose to engage in reduction.

Again we can ask the question of how.

2.1   The Gestalt Laws of Grouping

To answer this, we'll start with a consideration of the seminal work by Kurt Koffka in 1935, the Principles of Gestalt Psychology—a work still referenced heavily today in the fields of design. In fact the overarching Law of Good Gestalt is often used interchangeably with the Law of Prägnanz. According to the Gestalt Principles, depictions of sufficient data benefit from fewer rather than more elements, symmetric rather than asymmetric composition, and generally characteristics aligned with other principles and biases in human perception (aka Gestalt Principles of Perception). These include principles that emphasize what makes elements in visual depictions appear more related to each other (Gestalt Laws of Grouping) as well as, in contrast, what might allow individuals to more effectively compartmentalize when relevant; i.e. separate signals from noise, delineate units of analysis and generally systematically leverage meaningful distinctions via Figure-ground organization.

Law of Past Experience

Particularly reminiscent of the discussion of biases in Chapter 1 is the Gestalt Law of Past Experience. Essentially this law suggests that past experiences strongly color the way in which we categorize visual representations (e.g. of data). No big surprise there. In the simplest of examples, the law implies that if you have most recently seen data arranged in a particular manner (e.g. geographically), you are likely to group new data with comparable attributes (e.g. the net revenues of firms with off-shore headquarters) in a similar manner—even if doing so is not always ideal or appropriate. The closer in time the two depictions the greater the likelihood of this effect.

Past experience of course can have many pervasive impacts. Regular exposure to certain forms of visual representations will predispose audiences to certain approaches to interpretation, and even make alternative visual forms of visual representation appear less relevant. When used for the interpretation of data presented in bar-chart formats, for example, encountering data presented in a partially seemingly related format (e.g. scatter plots with error bars) can inadvertently lead to the reduction of meaning. Conversely, repeated recent exposure to graphical representations intending to depict association over time (say a line chart) might bias individuals in their interpretation of graphs that don't explicitly depict longitudinal associations (e.g. viewing the points on the right side of an X-Y scatter to be somehow more relevant/timely than those on the left). In such a case, past visual experience is introducing properties that don't actually exist, thus again detracting from interpretation.

At the extreme, in cases of depictions that do not easily translate into recently considered familiarized forms (e.g. network diagrams for those only recently exposed to pie charts), cognitive dissonance may trigger filtering such depictions in their entirety; "That's neat, but I think I'll wait for the next pie." Clearly there is something to be said for the virtue of varied exposure to visual representations, as well as the virtues of designing for easy transitions between visual artifacts. Inducing skips in visual examination is not something designers should shoot for.

Law of Proximity

Related to the Law of Past Experience, which focuses on how time can impact assumptions of relatedness, is the Law of Proximity, which focuses on how space can impact such assumptions. The law states that when individuals observe a set of elements (e.g. data points in a plot, sets of entire graphical idioms in a dashboard, etc.) they tend to interpret those close to one another as more related than those distant. Once again, this can be a useful bias provided those proximal items are in fact strongly and meaningfully related. However, our tendency to make spurious associations based on proximity, or at least perceived proximity, can also get us in trouble.

Take for example the case presented in Figure 2.1. In the left panel, a set of data is presented in an X-Y scatter plot along two of the perhaps many dimensions that the set may ultimately be characterized by. From the perspective of the left pane, the data appear as a continuous cloud with relatively Normal univariate distributions. This vantage point might reinforce a belief that the data in fact represents a single continuous population, and hence only a singular approach to modeling and decision consideration might be warranted.

However, a simple expansion of the view by a third dimension of the data (call it "Z") might put this homogeneity belief in question. The right panel in Figure 2.1 provides this vantage point. While the left panel can be thought of as an aerial view where the z-axis is coming out of the plane towards the viewer, the right panel rotates this data set to reveal only very tenuous connections between three subsets. The reality and relevance of this distinction only raises additional research questions that would need their own additional examination, but these are questions that might yield much greater intelligence; And ones that might have been ignored had this only slightly more nuanced vantage point not been considered.

Our biases, in some cases reinforced by much of what we are taught methodologically, have an insidious way of convincing us that exploration or even targeted checks for greater complexity is not necessary. We are often the worse for it.

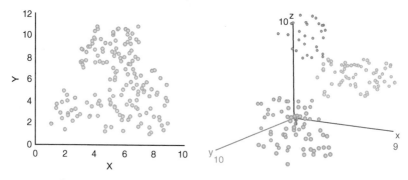

FIGURE 2.1 The Same Data: Proximity Bias as a Function of Dimensional Vantage Point

Law of Similarity

Clearly not all characteristics of data are defined by time and space. Other attributes describe the state of things. Physical properties might be captured in data as temperature, viscosity, weight; personal properties characteristic of individuals or organizations may include level of training, risk tolerance, altruistic tendencies, system criticality, etc. These attributes may also be the foundations of group associations that may or may not be real.

The Law of Similarity generally addresses this. It states that elements within a set tend to be grouped when their attributes (beyond timing and location) are comparable. Less comparable elements will tend to be excluded from such groups, perhaps being binned into their own distinct groups. The greater the similarity/ dissimilarity, the greater the likelihood of such groupings. Graphically the choice of renderings (color, iconography, etc.) may also serve as artificial attributes further complicating these grouping tendencies. This makes the selection of not only represented data and dimensional vantage points, but also the internal and relative forms of such representation, an extremely delicate one.

Consider the following example. A single data set, a single numerical dimension of that set in fact, is arranged by the alphabetical order of an associated nominal dimension. The first bar chart in Figure 2.2 provides the resulting depiction. In contrast, the right panel of Figure 2.1 presents that same data presented in a Pareto chart format (descending in numerical value). As difficult as it may be to believe, countless tests with human respondents show that in the first case individuals are much more likely to see two groups in the first panel. This curious tendency and those revealed by other tests of the Law of Similarity show this phenomena to transcend the professional backgrounds of those viewing such idioms.

Law of Symmetry

Human beings evolved to recognize, and indeed depend on, certain regularities in nature. One of these is symmetry. Most of the living organisms we have learned to interact with demonstrate significant symmetry in at least their external

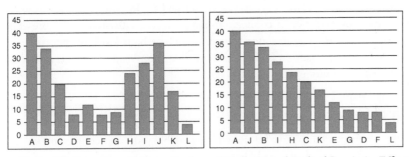

FIGURE 2.2 The Same Data II: Complications of Similarity and Ordinal Proximity Effects

appearance. Many demonstrate bilateral symmetry being approximately equal on either side of a line (the sagittal plane in biology). Some have more complex symmetrical forms such as radial or rotational symmetry (think starfish but also plants).

Symmetry also exists in the non-biological natural world. We encounter symmetry in everything from that which is visible at the atomic level, to the just naturally visible (e.g. snowflakes), to the massive (think the generally spherical or rotational structure of astronomical bodies). Our own architecture and the design of everyday consumer goods are permeated throughout with centuries of social evolution influenced by symmetry. Everything from toothbrushes to airplanes to skyscrapers.

In short, we are used to symmetry. We have come to expect it. As a result, sometimes we assume it exists even when it does not.

How does this relate to our natural tendencies when it comes to interpreting visual representations of data? Designing for that interpretation? The Law of Symmetry recognizes the mind's tendency to anticipate symmetry around a central point, line or plane. In the absence of sufficient presentation (e.g. presenting only the upper half of a distribution beyond a critical level), we will tend to fill in the blanks with reflection. However, and particularly relevant to the way in which audiences may reduce overly complex visual presentations, the law also suggests that when presented with two seemingly symmetrical visual artifacts the mind will have a tendency to connect them as a single whole.

Consider two plots. One showing how an outcome Y_1 is related to a managerially controlled independent factor X_1, another doing the same for an alternate set of factors Y_2 and X_2. Say that both of these depictions suggest significant positive relationships between the outcomes and the independent variables. Imagine showing these two graphs to a set of individuals and asking them a series of questions including the likelihood of synergies and tradeoffs existing in the pursuit of Y_1 and Y_2. Interestingly in simple experiments such as this, individuals appear much more inclined to assume synergies exist when the two trends are in the exact same direction (grouping by the Law of Similarity) and are much more likely to assume the existence of tradeoffs when the trends are in opposing directions (i.e. when the X_2–Y_2 trend line is an exact and opposite reflection of the X_1–Y_1 relationship). This is a fairly remarkable finding in that nothing is ever said of the relationship between X_1 and X_2, or Y_1 and Y_2. In other words, even in the absence of any evidence of connections between two subsystems, joint presentation and the existence of either high similarity or high levels of reflection can have very different (and in both cases misleading) implications on interpretation. Increasing proximity exacerbates this effect.

Law of Closure

In the previous example we witnessed the possible joint and contrasting impacts that multiple Gestalt Laws might have on the perception of data structure in visual data representations. Although focusing on structural perceptions, it is important to appreciate that these laws not only apply to static attributes in the sense of intrascopic Set Biases, the Gestalt Laws of Perception also extend to misperceptions akin to intrascopic Trend and Causal Biases.

The Law of Closure represents the embodiment of "how" in that it refers once again to the tendency of individuals to interpolate and extrapolate. This of course can happen both in low information as well as high information settings. The law itself is fairly generic, in that the manner by which closure takes place is not predefined it. Closure may borrow from symmetry, similarity, proximity or past experience in its accomplishment. It may also draw on other laws that associate in trends. To better appreciate the form that closure can take, especially in the context of data visualization, it is worth considering the more nuanced nature of its associated laws.

Law of Continuity

The foundations of the Law of Continuity are attributed to works of many historically significant research efforts, such as Johannes Kelper's work in trigonometric estimation, relevant to his study of planetary motion in the late sixteenth and early seventeenth century. Specifically the original Law of Continuity as later formally outlined by Gottfried Leibniz (1701) is stated as follows:

> In any supposed continuous transition, ending in any terminus, it is permissible to institute a general reasoning, in which the final terminus may also be included.

In other words, interpretations made of the finite can be used as the foundation for extrapolations to the infinite. The assumption here is that the finite that is examined is actually a subset of something infinite (or at least something significantly more extensive). The problem is that for most of the settings for which visual representations of data could be informative, infinite continuation isn't a very reasonable or useful assumption.

It's easy to come up with examples of why the Law of Continuity applied to a data visualization context could be problematic when insufficient data is presented. Our intrascopic biases towards linearity and continuity can lead us to draw some unreasonable assumptions about what might exist outside of a range depicted. If we didn't know any better and saw a graph of a positive relationship between the use of water and plant growth, a relationship that tends to be positive at least in the range of "very limited watering" to "moderate," we might suspect that this positive trend continues and that our best option would be to continue to add water. Of course there are downsides to excess that exist in almost all settings. Graphically, however, these downsides are not always apparent, and without sufficient counterbalancing experience we are apt to overwater things when we don't know any better.

In the context of overabundant data visualization, we can also be misled by our tendencies to see continuity where it might not exist. Take for example a stylized portion of a graphical network depiction of traffic flow as presented in Figure 2.3. In the left panel all flow through a node is shown simultaneously. If asked to extrapolate what might occur if inward flow of 12/min from due-West was reduced by half, the typical response would be that the outward flow of 12/min East would be reduced to 6/min. However a more fragmented (and realistic in this case) depiction would demonstrate that the assumption of linear continuity that led to this assumption was itself flawed. In the right panel, where the same information is provided, a slight adjustment supports greater clarity into what happens at the node.

The lesson from the Law of Continuity is that when an abrupt discontinuity exists in data and/or data relationships, one would do well to explicitly show it. Sometimes trying to do everything with a single visual makes comprehension a difficult task. System visualizations require systems of visuals.

Law of Common Fate

Similar to the Law of Continuity, the Law of Common Fate assumes that individuals may respond to exposure to movement paths of one type (e.g. graphics that show changes in state over time) and apply those same paths' characteristics to the interpretation of other depictions of change. As in the prior example, it is easy for movement to be a complex attribute for visual depiction. Complicating things is the option many designers engage in when attempting to make their visual artifacts interactive. In general this an option that makes a great deal of sense, but also one that can in itself mislead regarding the actual dynamics inherent to a data set. For example, permitting an individual to scroll through values of one variable X in an ordinal sequence, to observe associated values in Y, could be misleading if X cannot actually be modified linearly or only takes on fairly discrete and discontinuous levels.

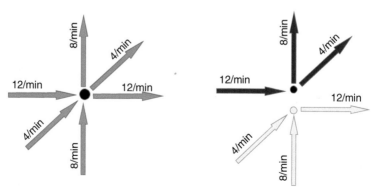

FIGURE 2.3 The Same Data III: Two Subsystems Merge and Continuity Misleads

The Law of Common Fate suggests that as human beings we have a tendency to assume a priori that transitions occur along smooth continuous paths—which is ironic given the abundance of discontinuity we explicitly build into the processes we manage. There have even been pupilometric studies showing this tendency to view movement and extrapolations of movement as continuing along smooth paths of progress. More to the point, in data visualization contexts, we can easily fall for the expectation that the kind of trends we observe in either static or interactive settings apply commonly across broad swathes of a data set. It lulls us into assuming systems are much less complex than they are. That the data might not actually consist of multiple fairly independent systems, and that one-size-fits-all solutions are our best solutions.

2.2 The Virtues of Good Fences

Let's take a step back for a moment. Yes, the laws just outlined are useful ones and demonstrate a reinforcement of the prior discussions of psychological biases and heuristics that play so powerful a role in the absence of sufficient data. They suggest these kinds of biases and heuristics can be just as dangerous in the presence of excessive data. In many cases, the visual representations of one data set need to be viewed as emblematic of a distinct system from that of another. In some cases even portions of larger systems are disparate enough to warrant consideration from distinct and overtly separate vantage points.

But sometimes sets of data or entire visual idiom systems really should be thought of as connected—because they *are* connected. Although designs must avoid spurious visual associations, there are many cases where design benefits from an ability to make visible both association and distinction. In fact some of the best visual designs are predicated on the ability to continuously reinforce association both explicitly and aided through perception-driven implication. It is therefore critical that we recognize tactics that are useful to ensure distinctions between elements in a visual representation can also be useful to emphasize the connectedness within subgroups of those representations.

These tactics are not without theoretical foundations themselves. Whereas the Gestalt laws discussed provide insights into how one might devise implied connectedness in visual designs, when that connectedness is real and relevant, they clearly also suggest kinds of distinctions that can help imply disconnectedness. Figure-ground organization, or the general ability to distinguish objects from their surroundings and highlight signals from noise, essentially relies on the success of these grouping laws as well as, critically, their failure.

Working backwards then, what kinds of demarcations can accomplish the kind of fences that reinforce separation where needed. The proximity principle suggests that if we want to ensure implied distinctions between groups of elements within visualization idioms or among a set of complete idioms, we would do well to create as great a spatial separation between such distinct groups relative to within-group distances as possible; a method not unlike the approach used by mathematical discretization and clustering techniques. However all of this must be done with a strong caveat. If otherwise distinct system data overlaps over a finite set of dimensions, in a single graph say, we can't simply change the data to appear otherwise. We can however present the two data sets in separate graphs. Designers should not force separation or proximity when such action actually distorts the reality of the data. Truthful presentation remains tantamount. We must pursue clarity, but always place truth ahead of these efforts.

According to the Law of Similarity, within-group association is facilitated by implied commonality. Most visual designers recognize this and distinguish unrelated elements that otherwise might appear similar by strikingly diametric colors or iconography, reinforcing the relatedness of those elements that are in fact directly related through common colors and iconography. The similarity of color schemes is of course complicated by the ability of individuals to distinguish between certain colors, and the still epidemic dominance of non-color printers.

Spatial placement of elements within individual idioms, as well as of such idioms within a larger system interface, can also help reinforce the true relationships present in data and deter latent tendencies towards misinterpretations. The Law of Symmetry provides some additional guidance here. For example, if it is likely that bilateral symmetry might be perceived horizontally between two otherwise unrelated elements, and if close proximity cannot be avoided (or serves other design purposes), simply configure them vertically. In certain contexts, a tendency to associate elements across a horizontal may exist regardless, but the consideration of additional effects in either direction due to misperceptions of symmetry is a useful design exercise. Another more overt option, that is not always possible without other issues in misperception arising, is to distinguish these elements by the amount of space they occupy in a system. Such differentiation breaks up symmetric association and reduces the likelihood of intrascopic Set Biases emerging from it.

Intrascopic Trend and Causal Biases can also be mitigated when the risk of misinterpretation appears high. As a case in point, there are several tactics for deterring inappropriate extrapolations of continuous linear trends into spatial regions where such trends cannot apply. These include the explicit depiction of strict practical or theoretical limits or cutoffs within the space of the graphic. If approaches to these limits are thought to be asymptotic, or taking on some other non-linear or discontinuous form, the embedding of a minigraph or sparkline can provide considerable guidance in interpretation (see dashed curves in upper right and lower right corners of left panel of Figure 2.4). In the case of multiple forms of dynamics captured by a data set, perhaps delineated by condition, subpopulation represented or region of examination, providing exemplar extremes as juxtapositions along with focal graphs can also reduce the likelihood of erroneous common fate assumptions (as per additional cases presented in right panel of Figure 2.4).

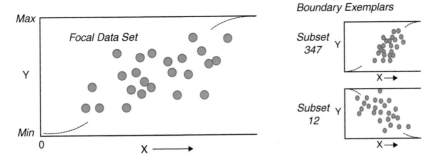

FIGURE 2.4 Deterring Trend and Causal Biases through Limit and Variance Awareness

And what about the first Gestalt Law of Groups we discussed: past experience? How can we counter that in a visual design? One approach would be to actually enable users to engage in new experiences with the data. This would guide intelligence and meaningful examinations of aspects of the data that are of the most interest to the audience. This suggests a certain level of dynamism in the design of visual artifacts and brings us to our closing discussion for this chapter.

2.3   Bifocals in the Forest

Ockham's Razor is often cited using the following phrase: "The simplest explanation is usually the correct one." Sadly much like many statements and claims attributed to people like Deming and Tufte, William of Ockham (c. 1287–1347) probably never said these specific words. At least we don't have any historical record of him doing so. What historians do have him on record for is: "Non sunt multiplicanda entia sine necessitate," or:

Entities must not be multiplied beyond necessity.

This suggestion applies equally well to data visualization design as it does to theoretical and empirical arguments. It implies that given the choice between functionally equivalent designs, the simplest design will tend to yield the best results in interpretation. It reiterates the Law of Prägnanz and the Gestalt Principles of Psychology, although predating these appreciably. Yet regardless of who's claim of "simple is beautiful" we chose to adopt, we must adopt with some precautions. Specifically we must adopt with a caveat referring back to the first chapter, remaining cautious regarding the threat of over simplification. The best visual designs reside in a middle ground. Design decisions must intelligently consider key features of audience and problem context, as well as required guidance and flexibility, towards effective use and understanding. They must include the "necessary" as well as the "sufficient" (to reference Goldratt 2000), just not the "excessive."

Accepting the fact that you as a designer can never fully anticipate the level of detail an audience might want along a specific data dimension can also lead to other health design practices: namely the enablement of drilling and satelliting mechanisms in visual data and decision support designs.

The idea of a "drill down" is well established. When there is a need for greater detail, strong visual representations permit such investigations. When broader perspectives are needed audiences are not forced to assemble a forest for the trees. The forest is already concisely presented. Users of even the most pervasive data manipulation systems are familiar with drilling down to better understand why anomalies in the broader picture exist (think Pivot and PowerPivot table drill-downs as outlined in Bendoly 2013). The efficient availability of these details on an as-needed basis helps audiences intelligently fill in the gaps in their mental models without being swamped in similar details that they may already understand well.

The opposite of the drill down—satelliting—is an equally valuable mechanism. It allows decision makers that are otherwise regularly tasked with work at a much more granular level to ask "what is the broader impact," the "system impact," of the action or event or property being studied? Satelliting is notably less common in modern data visual designs; in part because these broader holistic system-wide pictures are what they imply—extremely complex and often inclusive of issues beyond the knowledge base of the designers. Designs typically focus around what the user needs to know to maximize their effectiveness in their role, rather than what a user "should know" given that their actions are only part of a much larger system. Because of that, design requirements typically follow a drill-down path of a sort and seldom work their way up to higher levels of external impact.

This does not need to be the case. Although time and resource constraints on the development process do mandate some limits to scope, there is a growing understanding that a silo-oriented philosophy to a wide range of work and research settings is generally detrimental. What we do impacts others across both space and time; what we study is connected through space and time to the performance and actions of others as well. If we are to provide strong intelligence to guide actions through visualization techniques, we need to think at least about the most immediate recipients of the outcomes of these intelligently guided actions—otherwise the term "intelligent" won't be very meaningful. In short we should certainly focus on the principal audience and their needs in data visualization design, but we should also consider and enable them to consider at least a glimpse of the broader universe in which they are set. This requires a bit more sophistication than a single static monolithic depiction. Once again:

System visualizations require systems of visuals.

In the next chapter we will provide some concrete frameworks for managing this balancing act between providing efficient perspectives on the most critical data attributes for our audiences and providing them with sufficient (albeit non-blinding) richness for building deeper, more intelligent understanding.

References

Bendoly, E. (2013) *Excel Basics to Black Belt*, 2nd Edition, Cambridge, MA: Cambridge Press.

Goldratt, E.M., E. Schragenheim and C.A. Ptak. (2000) *Necessary But Not Sufficient*, Newark, NJ: Northriver Press.

Koffka, K. (1935) *Principles of Gestalt Psychology*, San Francisco, CA: Harcourt Press.

Leibniz, G.G. (1701) Cum Prodiisset…mss "Cum prodiisset atque increbuisset Analysis mea infinitesimalis…"; Printed in C.I. Gerhardt (ed.) Historia et Origo calculi differentialis G.G. Leibnitio conscripta, Hannover 1846; Translation in Child, J.M. (ed.) *The Early Mathematical Manuscripts of Leibniz*. Translated from the Latin texts published by Carl Immanuel Gerhardt with critical and historical notes by J.M. Child. Chicago, IL and London, England: The Open Court Publishing Co., 1920.

3

BEST PRACTICES IN VISUAL DESIGN

Elliot Bendoly

If individuals can be expected to have difficulty with both excessive as well as insufficient data presentations, clearly some middle ground must be sought out.

But how do we identify these middle grounds? How do we start?

Answering these questions requires an understanding of not only what the data in question might capture, what aspects of the data might be presented in a sufficiently but not excessively rich manner, what visual formats offer the capability of such presentation, but also, and critically, the fundamental intent of messaging to the target audience(s). In other words, it is difficult to imagine the message that a visual representation is designed to convey without a strong consideration of the audience targeted to receive that message; the context of both interpretation and application.

Because of this, whenever we discuss specific approaches to effective visualization we must think about the path from visual artifact, to interpretations of individual traits of a message and ultimately to the nature of consumed message Gestalt. This can be trickier than one might imagine. Even the most seemingly universal metric concepts as "percent profit margin" and "number of days in transit" can carry very different implications dependent on the audience context. Interpretation of such metrics, and their integration into an overall message, can differ by the extent to which individuals are focused on profit margin rather than social good or organizational learning; or by the extent to which timeliness is a virtue superior to quality or cost. If you attempt to inform individuals using measures that do not speak to them, or convey those measures by means that are flawed, their meaning is compromised. Indeed your messaging process as a whole is compromised, and the likelihood that your audience accurately comprehends the big pictures you would like to convey is greatly reduced.

3.1   Visualization as a Continuous Step-wise Process

Let there be no mistake, the interpretation of holistic messages is a process, with many opportunities for failure along the way. The design of a visual system of idioms intended to effectively convey those messages must critically account for these processes. The importance of process perspectives go beyond the design of individual artifacts, in part because the influence of visual artifacts can easily extend beyond their design intentions. Carl Weick's discussions on enacted sensemaking demonstrate that artifacts of actions taken in the process of attempting to understand an environment not only can solidify beliefs (aspects of mental models held regarding complex contexts) but can also fundamentally set the stage for future sensemaking efforts (Weick 1988, 2010). These subsequent efforts can in turn involve actions that derive subsequent influential artifacts. Increasingly, made possible through the growth in access to data and visualization capabilities, the artifacts that emerge from sensemaking efforts are visual ones. Because they can in fact set the stage for ongoing sensemaking efforts, its best to avoid digging holes of mis-messaging that only get harder to overcome with time.

Fortunately concerns over messaging are not entirely new. The field of Semiotics, going as far back as Plato and Aristotle by some accounts, critically considers the importance of fit between messaging intent and the means by which it can be accomplished. Some of the most important work on the relationship between the Gestalt of complex messages and reduced representational forms can be attributed to Charles Sanders Pierce (1839–1914). Pierce was an American mathematician, logistician, philosopher and scientist who ultimately became concerned with the process by which thought could be articulated, and subsequently with the process by which individual representational signs could be interpreted to convey ostensibly complex messages (cf. Pierce 1868, reprinted works 1958). Fundamental to his perspective was the distinction between representational signs, the interpretations they convey and the key reference traits that bridge the two. Recent considerations of best practices in visual design have capitalized on these distinctions (Amare and Manning 2008; Bendoly 2016). Figure 3.1, adapted from Bendoly 2016, provides an adaptation of Pierce's Semiotic Framework recently discussed in the management literature.

A modern interpretation of Pierce's framework in light of contemporary data visualization capabilities and managerial analytical interests, as above, makes evident the importance of distinguishing between the various structural characteristics of visual artifacts (last column in Figure 3.1) and the intended interpretation of messages to be conveyed (first column). It also emphasizes what emblematic data might be critical to such messages while simultaneously suitable to visual artifact development. Further it emphasizes that not all intended messages and audiences are created equal, and hence neither should associated visualization efforts. The first column in Figure 3.1 fairly plainly delineates between messages intending to be purely descriptive, from those that intend to convey some sense of predictive or perhaps even prescriptive implications.

Pierce's interest was in describing not only distinctions between these columns (respectively related to his use of the terms *interpretant*, *object-referent* and *sign*), but

Derived Meaning Targeted	Connection to the Object-Referent	Sign's Representational Characteristics
What are the properties and connections of the message you intend to convey?	*In what way are the properties of this message and their connections best represented?*	*What are the properties of depiction that capture these message properties?*
		1. Single attribute / Binning / Frequency / Density
	1. Analogy / Summary of central tendency / expected value	2. Multiple dimensions jointly depicted / rich-static snapshot
1. Demonstrating properties without association	2. Emblematic multidimensional subset / Facsimile of multiple rich observations	3. Comprehensive system depiction demonstrating dynamics of associations
2. Demonstrating association among properties	3. Replication of reality / Comprehensive facsimile connecting properties over time	
3. Supporting causal arguments explaining associations		

FIGURE 3.1 Pierce's Classic Semiotic Framework Applied to Management Data Visualization

also in the variety possible in each of these. His intent was to better understand how signs of a certain type were able to inspire certain forms of interpretation and not others. In particular he emphasized that simpler signs were fundamentally structurally constrained in their ability to capture aspects of meaning, and hence limited in their ability to convey holistic messages beyond a certain level of richness and complexity. In order to achieve such, more sophisticated and rich signs would be required. The prescription to the developers of visual artifacts thus harkens back to Chapter 2—we need to be wary of incomplete pictures. At the same time, we need to appreciate that some visual representations may be so overly complex as to confound and prevent the clear interpretation desired (Chapter 3). System visualizations require systems of visuals, but we don't always need to try to visualize an entire system in a single instance. Sometimes the messages we want to convey are much more compartmentalized. Sometimes we are better off when these messages are responsibly designed to be focused, not barring a more expansive view, but not starting with one.

In short, the adaptation of Pierce's framework in Figure 3.1 suggests that the most effective visualization efforts match message intent (target interpretant) to data-drive message characterization (aligned object-referent) to suitable and clear visual idiom forms (aligned sign characteristics). That is, the "middle ground" that we need to seek out for effective visualization efforts is really a matter of "matching" data selection and visual form to the message in question.

Is this seemingly straightforward step-wise approach effective? Do we have any evidence either way? Recent work provides some tantalizing empirical evidence to support how we not only may already be using this approach in some disciplines, but may also have been doing so for quite some time.

3.2   The Character of Data and Messages

In the previous chapters we have outlined many examples in which problematic extrapolations stemming from intrascopic Set Biases, Trend Biases and/or Causal Biases might emerge. Although useful to leverage concrete examples, it is also important to recognize that data visualization idioms consist of attributes that focus on specific data properties and imply the intent (or perhaps in some cases the happenstance) of fairly specific domains of messaging. These attributes are fundamental building blocks, albeit often obscured in visual representations, which can be common to a wide host of idioms. To get a greater appreciation of what these fundamental attributes might be and how they might relate to prior discussions of intrascopic biases and Gestalt Laws of Perception, we benefit from organizing these attributes in a framework of reference.

Figure 3.2 presents what is referred to as the Standard Convention in data visualization idiom design and interpretation (as adapted from Bendoly 2016). It

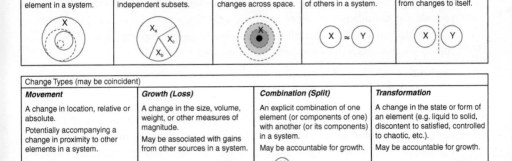

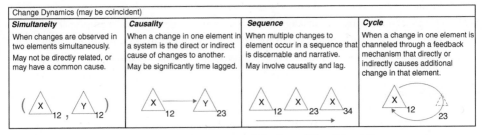

FIGURE 3.2 Representational Foci in the Functional Design of Data Visual Representations

is presented as a framework for classifying such depicted attributes in business data visualization efforts. We can discuss each general category (row) in this framework, as they increase in complexity and largely mirror increases in sign sophistication (i.e. proceeding downward in the far right column of Figure 3.1).

Static Traits

To begin with, the most commonly encountered visual renderings tend to be dominated by what we can classify as *static* traits. These often involve relative or absolute comparisons of specific elements, or simply measures of such elements in a system with respect to a measurement medium (e.g. a graduated y-axis). The choice of these renderings can be highly informative in detailing a system, but can also inform us about the Set Biases of the developers of these visuals—and can inappropriately direct or reinforce Set Biases held by audiences.

Construction

Depictions of construction capture the general shape, order and patterns observable in static snapshots of elements within often-larger systems. Think machine blueprints, government (state borders) or transit maps (roads, rivers); or think ordered organizational hierarchies, or non-directional social network maps, or maps outlining legal oversight on contractual claims. Spatial positioning is only one means by which to detail construction in other words. These renderings can provide the foundation of more sophisticated, directional, process implications (e.g. Gantt charts often accomplish this) but for the great majority of these structural depictions such dynamics are often not captured.

Segmentation

Related to depictions of construction, and often coincident, are depictions of static segmentation. These depictions notably describe how elements can be subdivided conceptually, but often do not detail position, organization or ordinality. These depictions are therefore in some sense more generally applicable, albeit also more prone to misuse—take for example the many instances of poorly applied pie-charting. Common traps in segmentation depictions are failures in figure-ground ratios, where critical elements are overshadowed by others in scale. These depictions often also imply equivalent levels of continuity or distinction among constituent elements. Particularly when the elements in question are difficult to tangibly define, strictly static segmentation depictions used in isolation can prove misleading.

Distribution

Many elements in real-world systems have characteristic distributions that are associated with them. The occupation of land by a population, the various levels of monthly demand for an SKU historically observed, the levels of conformance quality observed in a manufacturing process. Understanding these distributions allows us to better manage the deployment of resources, capacity and investments; permitting us to hedge against risk, but also set service level and operational efficiency and cost expectations. Depictions of distributions can be rich, but too commonly they are overly simplified and again prone to misleading interpretation. Take for instance the common use of bubbles to depict regional demand, population or event frequency/intensity on a geographic map. More often than not, such bubbles sizes do not actually relate to area-of-effect; but in cases in which they do, the implied even, symmetric continuity of that effect can lead to misguided assessments. Misleading representations of distribution tend to increase as the dimensionality of the distribution increases. In an area-of-effect example we have typically two dimensions to cover. But misrepresentations can occur even in unidimensional distribution depictions. For histograms there remain risks that excessively broad binning based on symmetry/continuity assumptions can mask relevant bimodalities for instance.

Similarity (dis-) and Boundedness

Implied in depictions of constructions, segmentation and distribution is the ability to distinguish between individual elements, portions of elements or states that elements can take on within a system. Occasionally, distinctions between a subset of elements, motivated by measurement differences in many cases, are the focus of static depictions (rather than how any one element fits into a whole). Similarity (dissimilarity) depictions often focus on juxtaposing a few, often only two, elements along some measurement criteria; Think the many two-bar charts that attempt to demonstrate how much greater one category/country/policy/technology performs/costs relative to another. In some cases, proxies for distribution are included to depict the extent to which these differences tend to be relevant (think box-plots); and in some cases the focus of the depiction in fact is in the distinctiveness of such elements. The depiction of boundaries between elements, either in the form of legal territorial boundaries, boundaries describing crystallography or organic morphology, boundaries distinguishing social groupings— these can all form the foundation of story-telling that, like many static depictions, can be augmented by additional visual forms. Once again, the lack of further representation can be entirely suitable, but it can also give us a window into the biases of the developer of these renderings.

Change Types

As alluded to, while the depiction of static traits may lay the foundation for richer visual representations, something else needs to be present for such richness to exist. Stated plainly, what is required is a second representational form or embedded depiction, indicative of changes that have, will or even "may" take place with regards to the elements focused on. These changes may be depicted coincident with shifts in time or other variables. However, change depictions in and of themselves need not attempt to, and often are best designed intentionally not to, capture causality. Like static trait depictions, they may lay the ground-work for richer change dynamic depictions, getting at the manner by which change occurs, but change type depictions are fundamentally about what the changes "are."

Movement

Depictions of the movement of elements across some physical or conceptual space are some of the most common renderings of change in management. Here we have countless examples of directional flow in supply chains captured, or direc-tional flow of communication or trust in social networks for that matter. In indus-trial processes, we superimpose upon process flowcharts the planned and actual direction and magnitude of flow. In understanding political and economic shifts we often superimpose the flow of voting trends and consumer populations. In the design of advanced materials we superimpose directional indicators of surface texture, or field lines in the case of magnetic properties. Pointing the way that elements move in systems can tell us a lot about what to expect, albeit not neces-sarily telling us why. In this sense, we are apt to expect that general directional trends are trends written in stone, rather than dynamics in themselves and subject to controlled change—here designers have to be careful of being misled by their own inherent intrascopic Trend Biases as well as having such biases mislead their audiences in extrapolation.

Growth and Combination (split)

Movement of course isn't the only change relevant in describing elements in sys-tems. Understanding the growth (or loss) that elements can experience in terms of value, capabilities, multiplicity and even variance can be invaluable. Equally valuable are depictions that describe the manner in which multiple elements come together to form a whole; i.e. the general direction by which components combine to form what would otherwise be shown only as finished or intermedi-ate products in a static construction. Along with these depictions is the potential to refer to limitations/constraints in growth and loss, as well as economies and diseconomies that accompany such changes. The loss of material in the process of combining two elements for example, or the manner in which goods of a variety of shapes create complications in warehousing or vehicle packaging, or the dependency that individual project steps may have on preceding value added efforts—all of these can be represented visually to allude to (albeit not definitively identify) critical bottlenecks faced in systems, inefficiency and resource underuti-lization, and therefore can provide fertile ground for process and system improve-ments. As with depictions of movement however, these can often benefit from a little insight into why losses might be taking place, why combination or growth happens the way it does, why certain bottlenecks are active in some cases and, at least seemingly, not others.

Transformation

Last, change is often not something that can easily be measured by tangible quantity or location. Sometimes the most important changes relate to transformations in key elements of a system. Consider shifts in process runs from manufacturing, to cleaning and/or maintenance, or shifts in project work from low to high priority, transitions from pre- to post-implementation operations around changes in quality programs or information technology, or shifts in organizational culture after mergers, new leadership and training. Each of these changes might seem difficult to capture using the same visual forms that would otherwise seem natural for capturing movement or growth. However all of these changes have a host of dimensions that might actually be measureable. It may be that a sufficient understanding of such changes requires multidimensional comparisons of contrasting states. What remains difficult however, as in other cases, is avoiding traps in which certain changes are erroneously attributed to specific causes (e.g. the presence of a technology, the use of training programs, the introduction of a new CEO) when those changes are really just a natural progress due to other factors at play.

Change Dynamics

Where depictions of change provide tantalizing suggestions regarding the manner in which change takes place and the kinds of levels of magnitude and relative positioning that elements in a system might take on, depictions focusing on change dynamics are concerned fundamentally with attempting to explain why it is that these changes occur; or at least richer representations of processes describing how these changes emerge.

Simultaneity

The most unassuming of change depictions are those that simply attempt to demonstrate changes across multiple elements and/or dimensions that occur simultaneously across time. Responsible depictions of association must strongly emphasize that the intent is not to imply causality. These depictions might be the foundation for further investigating the possibility of causality, but if their premise is purely to provide a faithful representation of simultaneity, associated descriptive verbiage must be clear on this point. Often line plots of two factors in a single or double y-axis configuration, with time along the x-axis, have this very intent in mind. However without cautionary notation specifying that these are simply coincident measures in time (if they are in fact that), it is easy for an audience to fall into intrascopic Causal Bias traps.

Causality

On the other hand, if processes are well understood, or if evidence from controlled consideration has demonstrated that certain actions or changes in elements mandate other dynamics, there may be reason to strongly depict causality in related visual depictions. In such instances, associated verbiage goes a long way to emphasizing that certain changes in Y are a direct or indirect (but anticipated) reaction to changes in X. In some instances reinforcement of causal relationships is aided by process diagrams (e.g. emblematic flow charts) accompanying depictions of metric relationships (e.g. scatter plots).

Sequence

Indirect causal relationships and non-causal associations are not always easily depicted in line or scatter plots, however. And in some instances the intent of a message is not to attempt to describe how changes to one element associate with changes in others. In some cases the rich story that needs to be told is the step-wise progression that a single element undergoes as a function of internal processes. Consider the progression that takes place in 3D printing processes. Consider the various states of social media activity around popular ad campaigns, or the manner in which traffic ebbs and flows in an amusement park, or at an entertainment event or medical facility. Comparing a couple of before and after measures does do justice to the true nature of change taking place in these settings. More effective depictions rather come in the form of multiple, multidimensional snapshots of change over time. Increasingly we see these depictions provided in the form of simulated, reenacted or even directly recorded time-lapse images or video; with the option of play-back speed and vantage point placed in the hands of the audience.

Cycle

Further complications in many processes are introduced by recursive mechanisms, such that a change in one element results in changes in the very factors that appear to have caused it in the first place. Feedback loops are the engine behind many system dynamics models, and appropriately so, since such loops can be so fundamentally influential in the dynamics of real-world systems. As in the case of internal sequence depictions, multiple snapshots are required to capture the role of feedback mechanisms. Both timing and direction are critical in depictions. Further useful are summary depictions juxtaposing the manner in which changes in X influence Y, against the manner in which changes in Y influence X. Static causal loop diagrams are often the foundation of effective cycle depictions, but fall short in and of themselves in capturing what are often intended messages regarding system dynamics. Because of this, the most effective cycle depictions leverage both renderings of overall system connections (Causal Loop Diagrams—CLDs) as well as multiple simultaneous multi-period time plots that individuals can specify; with added advantage again given to the availability of play-back speed options. Plots showing multiple factors as they co-evolve overtime, e.g. scatter plots with points distinguished by color or transparency, or augmented simulation environments, can further emphasize the manner in which changes can feed off each other in systems. Once again: system visualizations require systems of visuals.

3.3 Fit between Intent and Design

Now let's take a step back and consider once again Pierce's Semiotic Framework as it applies to the Standard Convention attribute set we just discussed. If the rows in the Standard Convention are in some way comparable to levels in the last column of Pierce's Framework, we should expect that overtime some of the most effective visualization applications, in terms of their ability to successfully convey intended meaning, will have become apparent in practice. Figure 3.3 suggests that this may be the case for several established visualization techniques in management.

Control Charts, for example, have continued to see extensive application in practice, not because they are complicated, but because they are limited in scope

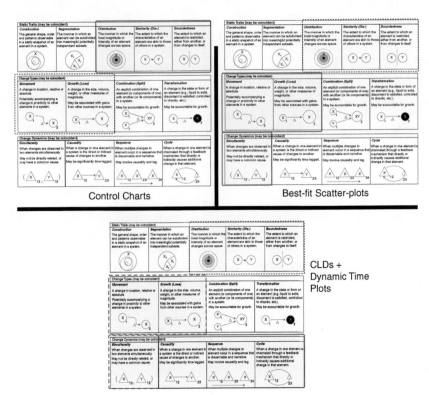

FIGURE 3.3 Plot Characteristics Supporting Matched Structures in Pierce's Framework

to match messages that are similarly limited in scope. They fit their application. Similarly, scatter plots with best-fit line estimates intended to describe trends and association have remained popular and often highly informative (provided claims regarding emulated causality are very cautiously tempered). CLD and developments in highly flexible dynamic time renderings are also coming into their own. As highlighted in Figure 3.3, focal traits of these different visual idioms leverage increasingly richer visual conveyance and are aligned with increasingly richer messaging intent. Bendoly (2016) discusses the alignment of these particular visual choices with visual intent in greater depth, though it is sufficient to emphasize that vastly different approaches have proven successful given particularly different purposes.

Control, Flexibility and Enacted Sensemaking

As noted earlier, well thought-out visual designs can fulfill current needs as well as provide a strong foundation for continued learning about complex systems to be managed. Discussions of the role that dynamic user interfaces can play in developing a rich interpretation of data are therefore only the beginning of what effective user interfacing can yield. What happens when a user is suddenly able to not only look at a static visual artifact but easily manipulate the scope of the visual to focus on something, or easily filter out certain observations, or modify the vantage point so that different variables are compared as they co-evolve over time? What happens when they are given the ability to superimpose boundaries between subsets of data and ask an application to determine the extent to which such subdivisions are statistically relevant across other dimensions? What happens when individuals are able to easily annotate what they believe they are learning in their interpretation of data on the very graphical renderings they are working with, and are able to share their collective thoughts with others for follow-up discussion (in real time or in any case whenever they would like)?

> System visualizations require systems of visuals.

The best systems don't just enable the interactions between users and software interfaces. Those very interactions are part of these systems as well, and hence something worth our attention in design. As in Figure 3.4, the pursuit of crisp systems that permit both interfacing along standard schema as well as customization, walking the fine line between under-specification and excessiveness in data presentation, is not outside our grasp in design.

Users create artifacts that capture their perspectives on the visualized data. Yes, those perspectives may be affected by their own internal biases, and yes their interactions may be influenced by the biases of the designers of the visual environments manipulated, but they are adding to a dialogue. And provided organizations encourage the voicing of different perspectives, these shared perspectives can be scrutinized, countered, reinforced or even dismissed. But they can also give

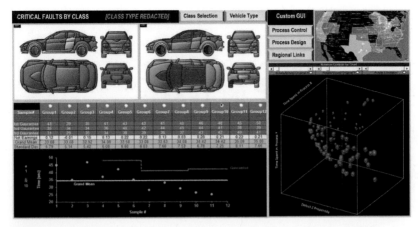

FIGURE 3.4 Quality Control System of Visuals in an Interactive/Customizable Dashboard Format

rise to subsequent visual consideration, more targeted evaluations, and additional requests to redevelop and enhance the visual platforms that the organization leverages. The process of attempting to make sense of a complex system gives rise to new ideas and artifacts that facilitate further sensemaking (Weick 1988). The most effective organizational sensemaking processes moving forward are going to continue to depend on open lines of communication and critical thinking. An organization that embraces flexibility in visualization tools, control by the prospective audiences over specific forms of renderings, and guards users against the risk of cognitive overload by establishing best practices in rational connections between intent and visual form, are going have the most meaningful discussions on tool design and are likely to reap the most benefits from visual system use.

References

Amare, N. and A. Manning (2008) "A Language for Visuals: Design, Purpose, Usability," *Conference: Professional Communication Conference*. IEEE International.

Bendoly, E. (2016) "Fit, Bias and Enacted Sensemaking in Data Visualization: Frameworks for Continuous in Operations and Supply Chain Management Analytics," *Journal of Business Logistics* 37(1): 6–17.

Pierce, C.S. (1868) "On a New List of Categories," *Proceedings of the American Academy of Arts and Sciences* 7: 287–298.

Pierce, C.S. (1958) *Collected Papers, Vol. 1–6*, edited by C. Hartsborne and P. Weiss. Cambridge, MA: Harvard University Press.

Pierce, C.S. (1958) *Collected Papers, Vol. 7–8*, edited by A.W. Burks. Cambridge, MA: Harvard University Press.

Weick, K. (1988) "Enacted Sensemaking in Crisis Situations," *Journal of Management Studies* 25(4): 305–317.

Weick, K. (2010) "Reflections on Enacted Sensemaking in the Bhopal Disaster," *Journal of Management Studies* 47: 537–550.

4

SUSTAINING COLLECTIVE SENSEMAKING IN TEAMS

Five Patterns of Interaction

Alice Comi, Martin Eppler and L. Alberto Franco

How can meeting facilitators sustain collective sensemaking in management teams? Management scholars have recently called for the development of a "meeting science" (Allen et al., 2015), which examines how managers interact in such gatherings, and how their collective sensemaking can be better supported (Schuman, 2005). Accordingly, a concern for articulating guidelines for facilitators of team meetings has rapidly gained traction. This work has resulted in two broad types of prescriptive frameworks: *competence* and *design*. *Competence frameworks* characterize the skills and knowledge that facilitators should possess to best do their work (e.g. Azadegan and Kolfschoten, 2012; Gregory and Romm, 2001; Hunter and Thorpe, 2005; Kaner, 2007; Lieberman Baker and Fraser, 2005; Schein, 1998, 1999; Schwartz, 2002). *Design frameworks*, on the other hand, are those that offer guidelines for the design and conduct of facilitated team meetings (e.g. Ackermann, 1996; Kolfschoten et al., 2007; McFadzean and Nelson, 1998; Phillips and Phillips, 1993; Schein, 1998; Wardale, 2013).

The work presented in this chapter is aligned with the latter type of frameworks. In developing our facilitation guidelines, we built on the suggestion that visual representations such as diagrams, drawings and sketches stimulate cognition and collaboration. The visual has since a long time ago been recognized as being worth a thousand words (Brisbane, 1911; Larkin and Simon, 1987; Bendoly, 2016); and has become increasingly widespread in modern organizations – also thanks to the diffusion of computers, tablets and smartphones (Bell et al., 2013; Meyer et al., 2013). By focusing on visual facilitation, we extend current *design frameworks* to improve understanding of the links between behavior and visualization in meeting settings.

In order to address our research question (how can meeting facilitators sustain collective sensemaking in management teams?), we have analyzed a large set of data (consisting of field observation, one-to-one interviews and first-hand experience of visual facilitation) and iterated back-and-forth from data to theory (Orton, 1997). Through this analysis, we have identified five patterns of team interaction that are conducive to collective sensemaking, and we have worked out how visual facilitation can initiate and sustain such patterns—which we have labeled as *scoping, mediating, fluxing, de-boxing* and *re-appropriating*. We have then striven to make our findings applicable by meeting facilitators, through development of guidelines that are meant to provide a conceptual language (rather than being strict prescriptions).

4.1   Appreciating the Audience and Context

By working in an action research mode with more than 40 management teams in the last five years, we have experimented with visual facilitation as a means to initiate and sustain collective sensemaking in management meetings. The majority of teams represented the for-profit sector, although we do have assorted experience in facilitating teams working in the not-for-profit sector. The number of participants in a given facilitated meeting ranged from five to fifteen, with a typical size of eight. The duration of facilitated meetings varied from one hour (minimum time) to two-day workshops (maximum time). Facilitated meetings were typically attended by managers working for the same organization; although some meetings involved participants drawn from different organizations. From a content perspective, meeting participants tackled issues ranging from business models, to innovation (i.e. product, service and process) and strategy (e.g. alliance, marketing or R&D strategy). This makes for a very broad and diverse corpus of data on visual facilitation experiences. We believe that this diversity leads to greater validity in generalizing from observed phenomena to interaction patterns and facilitation approaches.

Overall, our dataset is comprised of a combination of meeting video-recordings, photographs, visual outputs, observation notes, as well as transcripts of one-to-one interviews with meeting participants. Data analysis to develop interaction patterns and facilitation approaches followed an iterative–inductive approach that required iterating back-and-forth between theory and data (Orton, 1997). This type of analysis entailed engagement in extensive discussions concerned with making sense of the collected data, as well as exploring different ways of structuring and representing it. Indeed, working together on data analysis allowed us to "play" with the data in order to be both rigorous and creative. First, we independently reviewed collected data, and identified any data item for which we felt that we could make a sustainable argument with respect to a distinctive team interaction pattern. This process was partially informed by the literature on facilitated workshops supported by the use of visual aids. Next, we engaged in discussion among the three of us about each relevant data item. These debates ensured theoretical sensitivity (Strauss and Corbin, 1998), and involved clarifying the meanings of data items, together with their potential clustering and linkages. Finally, interaction patterns emerged and were refined by going back to the relevant literature. We discuss these below.

Scoping

One of the key challenges of team meetings is to delineate what should and should not be the focus of discussion (Mengis and Eppler, 2008). This is far from banal, as drawing boundaries around an issue has been shown to be difficult for management teams (Senge, 2006). Whether they discuss data that is either largely codified or characterized by rich latent knowledge; the scoping problems that they encounter echo the points made in Chapter 2, "Coping with Haystacks." Visual facilitation can provide management teams with ways to iteratively define the scope of their meetings, and make changes in such scope visible. This entails defining the boundaries of discussion visually, by distinguishing on-topic and off-topic themes. This also involves expanding, rather than restricting, such boundaries to encourage exploration of more themes (especially at the beginning of a meeting). A visual approach to scoping, thus, consists of using demarcation lines that nevertheless remain flexible (should there be a need to include other themes in the discussion). Such an approach is inspired by the Gestalt "Law of Closure" (see Chapter 2). By drawing a (relatively flexible) lasso around a set of data, the facilitator and participants can scope their discussion. An example of the use of visual facilitation for scoping is a simple visual agenda drawn on a flipchart. The facilitator may sketch the sequence of themes to be discussed on the flipchart so as to allow participants to suggest additions. In this way, the scope of discussion can be negotiated at the beginning of the meeting.

Mediating

A risk of any team meeting is that the discussion may turn into an unproductive conflict, focusing on egos rather than issues (Weiss and Huges, 2005). Mediating is an important form of collective sensemaking, which enables a team to make conflict productive by shifting the focus from people towards issues. To promote issue-oriented discussion (instead of people-oriented conflict), it is recommended making the visual center-stage so as to absorb the criticism normally directed at people (Black and Andersen, 2012; Mengis and Eppler, 2006). Directing criticism at elements of a drawing rather than at people, in fact, has been shown to improve the climate of a conversation and make conflicts more productive. As an example of the mediating effect of visual facilitation, think of two alternative options that are being discussed in a team meeting. Without visualization, they may become associated with the individuals arguing most adamantly for their case. However, as they are visualized (e.g. as a decision tree), the discussion shifts on further options that become possible as a result of the two options being discussed.

Fluxing

One recurring challenge in team meetings is the tendency to prematurely close debates and make decisions before hearing all relevant alternatives, or validating the identified possibilities. This "premature closure" phenomenon (Von Krogh and Roos, 1995) has been shown to be detrimental to the analytic quality of meetings in many management contexts. Fluxing, by contrast, is the ability of a team to sustain sensemaking until a higher level of collective understanding has been achieved. It is the team's ability to accept provisional progress, and remain flexible in its interpretations and deliberations. Visual facilitation has proven useful to keep the conversation in flux, especially through use of sketches (Henderson, 1991), which enable participants to flexibly adjust their representations as the conversation progresses. As compared to more "inflexible" visuals (such as PowerPoint), "flexible" sketches afford for completion, deliberation and exploration of alternatives. Making the visual look unfinished, thus, is an important aspect that can improve the quality of management meetings. As an example of the power of visuals to keep conversations in flux, imagine a horizontal timeline that is hand-drawn in a project meeting. Because of its provisional look and feel, it can keep the participants engaged in refining their plans to a greater extent than a polished PowerPoint slide.

De-boxing

With the term "de-boxing" we refer to an interaction pattern where teams think "out of the box" and go beyond categories that have been established through use of a certain framework or model (see also Kaplan, 2008 on cognitive frames; and Chapter 1 on "Incomplete Pictures," this volume). De-boxing is a spontaneous act of re-framing a problem or issue by extending or radically revising the terminology available to describe it. While the labels of visual templates (such as SWOT matrices, Gantt charts and BCG matrices) help meeting participants to stay focused on the most important issues at hand; these labels can also impose mental constraints that are counter-productive to collective sensemaking (Jarzabkowski and Kaplan, 2015). In fact, the template may constrain participants' thinking and lead to self-censoring or to withholding important information that does not fit the categories of the template itself. To overcome this "boxing" effect of any template, it is important (especially in a second step after having worked with the categories of the template) to help participants think "outside of the box" (i.e. outside of the template) and consider elements that are not afforded by the template, but might still be relevant for the discussion at hand. It can be one of the roles of the facilitator to enable participants to think beyond the categories of the template and modify its labels in accordance with the team's discussion. As an example, think of the well-known Porter's Five Forces framework that helps teams assess their position in a given market. This framework does not include considerations such as societal trends, regulation or technology breakthroughs. These, however, can easily be added visually as additional boxes or spheres.

Re-appropriating

As adaptive structuration theory (Poole and DeSanctis, 1990) has shown through a wide array of examples, (visual) artifacts (e.g. visual templates) are at times appropriated differently than anticipated by their designers. Yet "unfaithful" uses of a given artifact should not be blocked but instead encouraged (Sun, 2012). They can lead to more buy-in and ownership, as participants have made the artifact "their own" by re-appropriating it as they see fit with their purposes. They can also lead to more reflection and sensemaking (Griffith, 1999), insofar as they capture attention and trigger action on the part of team participants. Tweaking and adapting visuals to the requirements and constraints at hand is thus an important pattern to make visual facilitation serve the team to the best of its abilities. As emphasized in Chapter 3, "Best Practices in Visual Design," fit must continuously be re-evaluated as contextual needs adjust. As an example, think about the use of a Gantt chart, not as a visual project-planning tool, but as a visual staff workload device to check who may be overloaded.

4.2   Design Principles Applied

In this section we provide evidence of the use of visualization to facilitate the patterns introduced above, through a vignette from a real-world visually supported meeting and quotes from interviews with experienced managers. As it is not always possible to observe all five patterns within a facilitated meeting, the empirical vignette illustrates the occurrence of scoping, mediating and fluxing. Specifically, a *visual map* was used in a facilitated workshop held as part of a strategic review process at *Connect* (a pseudonym), a small company located in England. The company's mission is to enable disadvantaged individuals to get back into employment, by offering training and placement services. The purpose of the workshop was to help the top management team at *Connect* gain a shared understanding of the key strategic issues that the company was facing in 2007. The third author was invited to act as the workshop facilitator by the consultancy team conducting the strategy review for *Connect*. The visual map was developed "on-the-hoof" with the workshop participants, using the *Group Explorer* (www. phrontis.com/GE.htm) computer-supported mapping technology. Figure 4.1 shows the workshop setting.

The interaction excerpt below shows team members' discussion about the cross impacts between issues of "succession planning" and "company ownership." A snapshot of the visual map used during this part of the workshop is shown on the right-hand side of Figure 4.1. The excerpt illustrates how workshop participants—both facilitator (F) and team members (B, K and S)—mobilize and

Workshop setting   Map excerpt

FIGURE 4.1 Workshop Setting and Map Extract

foreground the contents of the visual throughout their discussion. The relative salience of these visual-supported behaviors is established sequentially, moment by moment.

F: Is that (looks and points at map) related to the previous one somehow? Or is it an independent…?

S: I think it will be impacted. The thing for me is what we want to do is develop our people which I think that (points at map) says, but we know that the component … something that needs to be developed in the next three to five years, it will be magnified … is succession.

B: (looks at S) Yes.

K: (looks at model, then at S, then at model, then nods)

S: (looks at C, then points at map) So, they … they're interrelated. You could take them as separate components…

F: Sure, they're … they're interrelated…

S: … but they are interrelated.

F: Can we … can we explore that a little bit… I mean can I bring that material into the other … into the previous screen? Aahm just ah… (locates and brings contributions into map display).

S: (looks at F, then nods)

In the excerpt above, S begins to articulate his particular understanding about how "succession planning" and "ownership issues" may be related (lines 3–6). Team members highlight certain parts of the map by orienting to and pointing at it throughout their discussion. In addition, F locates particular contents of the map, and makes some of them "visible" and others "invisible" to team members (lines 13–15). By placing particular contents in or out of the map display, F uses the visual for *scoping* the boundaries of the discussion that follows. Note that this is visually and collaboratively achieved by all participants in the interaction, and in particular by F and S.

    S continues to articulate his perspective about the cross impacts between "succession planning" and "ownership issues" until this is challenged by C, who argues that these areas are separate rather than interdependent. It is worth noting that conflict triggered by having different perspectives on particular issues is actually expected within management meetings. What the excerpt below aptly illustrates is how a focus on the map ensures that the conflict is about the issues and relationships on display rather than on the people who advocate them. The excerpt starts with C surveying the different (number-tagged) issues displayed on the map (lines 17–21) and then challenging S's perspective (lines 22–23).

C: (looks at map) 39, 15 and 9 I say are different from that, (points at map) I can see what 43–43 is different from 39, 15 and 9 (looks at S then points at map). 39, 15 and 9 are do we sell, do we float, do we stay as we are, and that decision will be made at that time.

   It is separate from developing people or whatever else (looks at S and uses hands to indicate separation).

S: (looks at C, then at map) Do ... do ... do you not think that if 39 occurred that that would affect that? So you wouldn't change your succession planning in the knowledge that in 12 months' time you sell it.

The above excerpt illustrates how a sustained focus on the map is *mediating* the beginning of a conflict. A debate between S and C ensues, during which F makes changes to the map in order to capture the debate while ensuring that S, C and the rest of the team continue focusing on the map. In contrast with the first excerpt, the contents of the visual are foregrounded rather than mobilized in this excerpt.

   In the next excerpt, as C continues to elaborate on his views (lines 29–32, 34–37), S suddenly uses the map to surface the conditions upon which an accommodation may be possible (lines 38–39), which in turn causes a shift away from the original contrasting positions (line 40–41). Figure 4.2 helps to illustrate this excerpt.

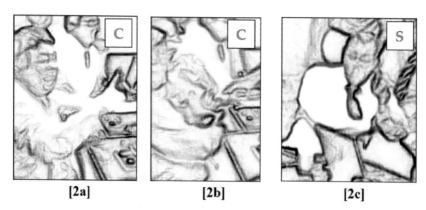

[2a]   [2b]   [2c]

FIGURE 4.2 Moving Towards Accommodation

S: (looks at map)

C: ...so (points at map) dependent upon the decision (uses hands) whether it's float, whether it's sale, whether it is management buyout, will depend on (points at map) how it can impact, it can impact in different ways (looks at F). [See Figure 4.2a]

F: (looks at C) Yes.

C: (looks at team, counts using fingers) One could be getting rid of you, one could be developing you further, and one could be taking over, (looks at S) management buyout, you become the shareholders (opens hands). [Figure 4.2b]

S: So those things (points at map, then looks at C) becoming in your way will be impacted on that. [Figure 4.2c]

C: (looks at map, then at S) In those ways (raises hands), in those three ways, dependent on the decision.

The preceding excerpt shows how the visual affords S the possibility of reaching an agreement which signals the emergence of a new collective understanding. When this happens, F makes changes to the map to highlight the achievement (lines 44–45, 51), as shown below in Figure 4.3.

F: (looks at map) Yes, so maybe the issue is the nature between, (looks at S) I mean the impact between these two "reds" (locates and looks at S while pointing at the two issues on map—now colored in red) [Figure 4.3a] will depend whether it is a buyout or (looks at C) it is a management sell-out decision.

S: (points and looks at map) It will change the shape of the things that you do within those comparisons. [Figure 4.3b]

F: (looks at S and nods)

C: (looks at S, then at map) that's the link.

F: (draws link) [Figure 4.3c]

 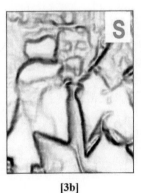 

[3a]   [3b]   [3c]

FIGURE 4.3 Making Changes to the Map

As already stated, the visual map referred to during the above interaction was built jointly with team members, and supported by the use of the *Group Explorer* technology. One of the characteristic features of this technology is that it enables team members to edit the contents of the map in "real time" as the discussion develops (this feature is typically available to the facilitator only, but it can be made open to all team members if needed). The high levels of editability afforded by the technology help those involved to keep the map always in transition. This supports the continuous *fluxing* of map content during team discussions, as evidenced in the preceding excerpts.

Table 4.1 provides additional evidence of the occurrence of *scoping, mediating, fluxing, de-boxing* and *re-appropriating*, gathered through our observations and experiences of facilitating meetings with visuals. This data consists of quotes from interviews with 30 experienced managers, conducted during a one-year ethnographic study within a large, multinational consulting company (with headquarters in the US, Germany and Switzerland). The informants commented on their use of sketches on flipcharts or pin-boards for interacting with clients. We use these quotes to illustrate how sketching, and not just computer-supported visual maps (as in the previous vignette), can sustain the five interaction patterns.

4.3   Lessons for Future Development

Based on our experiences, it is useful to delineate facilitation guidelines that contribute to collective sensemaking in teams. It is further useful to outline caveats regarding the potential downsides of such guidelines and possible corrective measures that can be taken in response. This is in line with recent developments in the facilitation field (e.g. Wardale, 2013); which emphasize encouraging reflexivity around recommendations rather than prescribing strict rules of conduct.

Scoping Visual Facilitation Guidelines

- Provide an out-of-scope visual area to "park" ideas that do not fit within set boundaries.
- Clarify conversation boundaries by adding visual tags to participants' contributions through color-coding or comments.
- Caveat: leaving the scope permanently up for discussion may make a meeting unproductive. It is important to close the scoping discussion after a certain time.

Mediating Visual Facilitation Guidelines

- Visualize controversial issues quickly, so that they become disconnected from an individual person; encourage and sustain the participant's attention on the visual.

TABLE 4.1 Additional Step-wise Evidence of Making and Sensemaking

---

Scoping:
• "Sketching is a stimulus to encourage a response from the client, especially because it's very hard for them to tell you what they want and don't want; when you sketch with clients it's sometimes easier to explain what you want by saying what it is not"
• "Sketching on the flipchart makes the notes visible for everyone so that the client can disagree, agree, or add to it, and you go let me just make it concrete, so I really understand you, and sketching is used as a cross-check device at the end of the meeting to reassure we have the same understanding of the situation and what must be
• "Sketching as mediation device for knowledge integration bringing together what the client thinks and what we think and develop shared understanding, knowledge verification ('did I understand you correctly that …') and you get a completely different input from the client when you sketch on a flipchart, you can consider it when developing a storyline and respect their concerns and point of view"

Mediating:
• "Sketching is more efficient than just talk, because it's essential and the other person disagrees with the sketch and not with me so that we are not having an argument, it's not a confrontational thing, the other person can actually see the argument"
• "The warmth of a sketch and openness of a sketch to convey something more congenial. Warmth means more expression from the person who has done the sketch and also more feeling/sense of the situation in which the sketch was developed"
• "With sketching I don't want to slay the client, I don't want to come across as a bulldozer or dogmatic, as someone who has arranged everything already, and I want the client to have the opportunity to not be overwhelmed and to be part of the game"

Fluxing:
• "With sketching, it will not look finished; it is not going to frighten me, and it is still open"
• "With sketching, you can feel unfinished in some way, in a good way, because you are in the process, things need to be able to move and change, you can say 'that's not it, let's cross that out', people feel happier, I see that you know we have learnt something"
• "Sketching helps you to understand a little bit more of details, because verbally you can say similar words, but we might actually be meaning something quite different by them. When you sketch, you realize whether or not you are talking about the same thing, it helps define some of the nuances which were not stuck there in your head as a perception"

De-boxing:
• "Sketching allows you and the client to be more creative but a sketch without PowerPoint might have them think that you haven't done anything"
• "Sketching is helpful when clients are stuck and cannot explain what they want because they haven't figured it out, then you can start to play around with them through sketching, you can start talking 'is it soft science or hard linear science?' and you use straight lines and curves to express the difference"
• "With sketching it feels like you are working together, it feels like in that hour's meeting, you are creating something together live; something that did not exist before the meeting is now there; the PowerPoint will be the same when you walk out as when you walked in, the client does not see their contribution"

Re-appropriating:
• "When you sketch the best is if people go 'oh no, that's not right', then you know they are active, they have understood what you are thinking and they are going to make it better; if they change it in some way, they not only understand, they actually adapt it, they own it"
• "With sketching it is all fresh and new, you are never going to be like 'here is a sketch I did a month ago', you are going to regenerate it every time; with PowerPoint you do not regenerate"

- Encourage people to visually modify elements that they criticize in order to improve them visually.
- Move comments to a neutral zone for subsequent deliberation and negotiation.
- Caveat: relying on a visualization to absorb conflict should not lead to the absence of conflict or to reducing accountability.

Fluxing Visual Facilitation Guidelines

- Employ sketchy markings and avoid polished looks.
- Reduce visual clutter and make sure people don't lose themselves in details.
- Highlight the current focus or position of the discussion so that people know where to contribute to at any given point in time.
- Caveat: towards the end of a discussion, commitments regarding the way forward need to be made. This should be reflected in a more definitive visual style that expresses the team's determination to follow-through on the discussed items.

De-boxing Visual Facilitation Guidelines

- Ask for other categories other than those provided by the template. Provide a space for comments on these categories, together with an appropriate visual attribute to identify them.
- Try different visual templates for the same context and switch between them to stimulate out-of-the box thinking (so as to go beyond the categories of a specific template). In other words, reiterate the mantra from Chapters 1–3: "*System visualizations require systems of visuals.*"
- Caveat: extending a given framework too much may lead to a loss of focus. This is a dilemma that the facilitator has to manage, by reflecting on the core mission of the team.

Re-appropriating Visual Facilitation Guidelines

- Ask for expected uses of a visual template. Allow spontaneous re-appropriations (don't stop "wrong" uses of a template right away).
- Think about different possibilities for interaction afforded by the visual, and implement them to suit the situation at hand.
- Caveat: overdoing re-appropriation may lead to abuse or inefficient usage of a given template or tool.

These guidelines are summarized and collectively contrasted alongside definitions and our empirical observations in Table 4.2.

Our work could be further extended in future research: first, the development of training materials (e.g. cards, handbooks and slides) based on actual use of the visual guidelines proposed here could provide facilitators with the opportunity

TABLE 4.2 Summary of Findings

	Definition	Benefit	Guideline
Scoping	Delineating the conversation limits *by visually demarking on-topic and off-topic areas*	Aligning the discussion	Visualize the boundaries as easily modifiable
Mediating	Reduce interpersonal conflict *by making the visual center-stage*	Making conflict more productive	Visualize controversial issues as provisional sketches and
Fluxing	Keep the conversation ongoing *by making the visual look unfinished*	Refining viewpoints and improving ideas and plans	Visually signal work in progress and keep it permanently visible
De-boxing	Help participants think out of the box *by going beyond the categories of a visual template (or switching visual templates)*	Considering all	Invite participants to think beyond the visual template by extending its categories
Re-appropriating	Stimulate ownership of solutions *by encouraging uses of the visual for purposes other than the ones intended by the designer*	Adapting the tool to situational needs	Allow for spontaneous re-uses of a visual template or framework to accommodate emergent needs

to rehearse. Second, visual facilitation guidelines could be developed to support meetings in which management teams go through special circumstances such as emergences or crises. While the dataset that we have used to develop our contribution is fairly broad, it does not cover such special circumstances, which may require a different set of team interaction patterns and visual facilitation guidelines. Finally, we have observed that sketching is particularly conducive to fluxing, but further research is needed to establish stronger associations between a given visual and a given pattern. Therefore, future research may focus on exploring which types of visual (e.g. diagrams, drawings and sketches) are most appropriate to sustain a given pattern.

References

Ackermann, F. (1996). Participant's Perceptions on the Role of Facilitators Using Group Decision Support Systems. *Group Decision and Negotiation*, 5(1), 93–112.

Allen, J., Lehmann-Willenbrock, N., and Rogelberg, S.G. (2015). *The Cambridge Handbook on Meeting Science*. Cambridge, MA: Cambridge University Press.

Azadegan, A., and Kolfschoten, G. (2012). An Assessment Framework for Practicing Facilitator. *Group Decision and Negotiation*, 1–33.

Bell, E., Warren, S., and Schroeder, J.E. (2013). The Visual Organization. In E. Bell, S. Warren, and J.E. Schroeder (Eds.), *Routledge Companion to Visual Organization*. London, England: Routledge.

Bendoly. E. (2016). Fit, Bias and Enacted Sensemaking in Data Visualization: Frameworks for Continuous Development in Operations and Supply Chain Management Analytics. *Journal of Business Logistics*, 37(1), 6–17.

Black, L.J., and Andersen, D.F. (2012). Using Visual Representations as Boundary Objects to Resolve Conflict in Collaborative Model-Building Approaches. *Systems Research and Behavioral Science*, 29(2), 194–208.

Brisbane, A. (1911). Speakers Give Sound Advice. *Syracuse Post Standard* (New York) March 28, 1911.

Gregory, W.J, and Romm, N.R. (2001). Critical Facilitation: Learning through Intervention in Group Processes. *Management Learning*, 32(4), 453–467.

Griffith, T.L. (1999). Technology Features as Triggers for Sensemaking. *The Academy of Management Review*, 24(3), 472–488.

Henderson, K. (1991). Flexible Sketches and Inflexible Data Bases: Visual Communication, Conscription Devices, and Boundary Objects in Design Engineering. *Science, Technology, & Human Values*, 16(4), 448–473.

Hunter, D., and Thorpe, S. (2005). Facilitator Values and Ethics. In S.P. Schuman (Ed.), *The IAF Handbook of Group Facilitation: Best Practices from the Leading Organization in Facilitation* (pp. 545–558). San Francisco, CA: Jossey-Bass.

Jarzabkowski, P., and Kaplan, S. (2015). Strategy Tools-in-Use: A Framework for Understanding "Technologies of Rationality" in Practice. *Strategic Management Journal*, 36(4), 537–558.

Kaner, S. (2007). *Facilitator's Guide to Participatory Decision Making* (2nd ed.). San Francisco, CA: Jossey-Bass.

Kaplan, S. (2008). Framing Contests: Strategy Making under Uncertainty. *Organization Science*, 19(5), 729–752.

Kolfschoten, G.L, De Vreede, G.-J., and Pietron, L.R. (2011). A Training Approach for the Transition of Repeatable Collaboration Processes to Practitioners. *Group Decision and Negotiation*, 20(3), 347–371.

Larkin, J.H., and Simon, H.A. (1987). Why a Diagram is (Sometimes) Worth Ten Thousand Words. *Cognitive Science*, 11(1), 65–100.

Lieberman Baker, L., and Fraser, C. (2005). Facilitator Core Competencies as Defined by the International Association of Facilitators. In S.P. Schuman (Ed.), *The IAF Handbook of Group Facilitation: Best Practices from the Leading Organization in Facilitation* (pp. 459–472). San Francisco, CA: Jossey-Bass.

McFadzean, E., and Nelson, T. (1998). Facilitating Problem-Solving Groups: A Conceptual Model. *Leadership & Organization Development Journal*, 19(1), 6–13.

Mengis, J., and Eppler, M.J. (2006). Seeing versus Arguing: The Moderating Role of Collaborative Visualization in Team Knowledge Integration. *Journal of Universal Computer Science*, 1(3), 151–162.

Mengis, J., and Eppler, M. J. (2008). Understanding and Managing Conversations from a Knowledge Perspective: An Analysis of the Roles and Rules of Face-to-Face Conversations in Organizations. *Organization Studies*, 29(10), 1287–1313.

Meyer, R.E., Höllerer, M.A., Jancsary, D., and van Leeuwen, T. (2013). The Visual Dimension in Organizing, Organization, and Organization Research: Core Ideas, Current Developments, and Promising Avenues. *The Academy of Management Annals*, 7(1), 489–555.

Orton, J.D. (1997). From Inductive to Iterative Grounded Theory: Zipping the Gap between Process Theory and Process Data. *Scandinavian Journal of Management*, 13, 419–438.

Phillips, L.D., and Phillips, M.C. (1993). Facilitated Work Groups: Theory and Practice. *Journal of the Operational Research Society*, 44(6), 533–549.

Poole, M.S., and DeSanctis, G. (1990). Understanding the Use of Group Decision Support Systems: The Theory of Adaptive Structuration. In J. Fulk and C.C. Steinfield (Eds.), *Organizations and Communication Technology* (pp. 173–193). Beverly Hills, CA: Sage.

Schein, E.H. (1998). *Process Consultation Revisited: Building the Helping Relationship.* London, England: Financial Times/Prentice Hall.

Schein, E.H. (1999). The Concept of "Client" from a Process Consultation Perspective: A Guide for Change Agents. *Journal of Organizational Change Management*, 10(3), 202–216.

Schuman, S.P. (Ed.) (2005). *The IAF Handbook of Group Facilitation: Best Practices from the Leading Organization in Facilitation.* San Francisco, CA: Jossey-Bass.

Schwartz, R. (2002). *The Skilled Facilitator: A Comprehensive Resource for Consultants, Facilitators, Managers, Trainers, and Coaches.* San Francisco, CA: Jossey-Bass.

Senge, P. (2006). *The Fifth Discipline.* Updated Edition. New York, NY: Currency Doubleday.

Strauss, A., and Corbin, J. (1998). *Basics of Qualitative Research: Techniques and Procedures for Developing Grounded Theory.* London, England: Sage.

Sun, H. (2012). Understanding User Revisions when Using Information System Features: Adaptive System Use and Triggers. *MIS Quarterly*, 36(2), 453–478.

Von Krogh, G., and Roos, J. (1995). Conversation Management. *European Management Journal*, 13(4), 390–394.

Wardale, D. (2013). Towards a Model of Effective Group Facilitation. *Leadership & Organization Development Journal*, 34(2), 112–129.

Weiss, J., and Huges, J. (2005). Want Collaboration? Accept and Actively Manage Conflict. *Harvard Business Review*, March Edition. Online at: www.hbr.com [accessed December 15, 2015].

5

PROCESSING DATA FOR VISUAL NETWORK ANALYSIS

Jukka Huhtamäki, Martha G. Russell and Kaisa Sill

The ecosystem concept has its roots in biology. *Collins English Dictionary* defines an ecosystem as "a system involving the interactions between a community of living organisms in a particular area and its nonliving environment." In business and innovation literature, the ecosystem concept is used both as a metaphor (e.g. Russell et al. 2011; Russell et al. 2015; Hwang and Horowitt 2012) and as a business strategy artifact (Moore 1993), as well as to refer to system-level analysis (cf. Pentland 2015).

To make a distinction between ecosystems of business and innovation in the context of this discussion, we point to their expected outputs. When the key objective in business ecosystems is to organize value creation and value appropriation in an interdependent and dynamic setting, we see the main benefit of innovation ecosystems as the increase of information flow and collaboration and therefore the creation of new business-relevant knowledge, ideas and technologies that may lead to new products, processes and companies. Innovation ecosystems survive through a constant idea flow, re-configuration, and evolution (cf. Pentland 2015).

Key characteristics of ecosystems are interconnectedness, interdependency, co-evolution, value co-creation, and co-opetition (Huhtamäki et al. 2011; Järvi and Kortelainen 2016). Actors in business ecosystems and innovation ecosystems are loosely interconnected: Iansiti and Levien (2004) stress that "like their biological counterparts, business ecosystems are characterized by a large number of loosely interconnected participants who depend on each other for their mutual effectiveness and survival." Success of a given innovation often relies on the success of focal companies' environments, i.e. companies are interdependent with each other (Adner and Kapoor 2010). Thomas and Autio (2012) state that co-evolving ecosystem actors "develop over time sympathetically with the other participants in order to maintain stability and health of the ecosystem in the face of change." Ramaswamy (2009) claims that value co-creation is an emerging business and innovation paradigm that leads to the need of "changing the very nature of engagement and relationship between the institution of management and its employees, and between them and co-creators of value—customers, stakeholders, partners and other employees." Finally, Ritala and Hurmelinna-Laukkanen (2009) note that co-opetition, i.e. collaboration with competitors, is in some cases "an effective way of creating both incremental and radical innovations, especially in high-tech industries."

Russell et al. (2011) take an even broader scope and define innovation eco-system as an "inter-organizational, political, economic, environmental and tech-nological systems of innovation through which a milieu conducive to business growth is catalyzed, sustained and supported." They note that in an ecosystem, individual relationships form a network structure "through which information and talent flow through systems of sustained value co-creation." The organic role of the network structure adds to the importance of the network as a visual idiom in visual analytics. The network view allows for making use of the Gestalt Laws of Grouping described in Chapter 1. Importantly, Russell et al. (2011) include organizational investors and individual people—founders, advisors and business angels—as innovation ecosystem actors (and therefore potential units of analysis in investigations) (cf. Huhtamäki et al. 2011). Impor-tantly, from a visual analytics viewpoint, all of these actors approach innovation ecosystems from their individual viewpoint, each of them with various biases in sensemaking.

In this chapter, we answer the call made in Chapter 3 to develop interactive visualization tools and collaborative visual investigation processes that enable the emergence of shared vision between innovation ecosystem actors and stakeholders (Russell et al. 2011). This process encourages the voicing of different perspectives that can "give rise to subsequent visual consideration, more targeted evaluations, additional requests to redevelop and enhance the visual platforms that the orga-nization leverages" and facilitates scrutinizing, countering, reinforcing and even dismissing those perspectives. We introduce a new visual and modeling idiom, namely the network, for empirical innovation ecosystem investigations in which the narrative is guided by scatterplots of country or industry-level aggregate metrics constructed from established KPIs (cf. Still et al. 2012). More broadly, this investigation contributes to the development of the overall the overall Informa-tion System artifact for innovation ecosystem analytics including i) technological artifact, ii) information artifact and iii) social artifact (Lee et al. 2015).

5.1 Ostinato Model: Visual Network Analytics for Innovation Ecosystems

Information visualization is an integral part of the network analysis methodology. In reviewing existing work on visual network analysis, Freeman (2000) notes that visualization both allows investigators to observe and identify patterns in social structures and also supports sharing these findings with others. Visual analytics (Wong and Thomas 2004; Keim et al. 2010) extends information visualization to include the processes of visualization-centric investigations. Computational approaches permit automating various phases of the analysis process.

Data-driven visual network analytics is a key method for supporting management and decision making through investigations of structural patterns latent in innovation ecosystems and social media phenomena. The Ostinato Model, a process model for data-driven visual network analytics, defines a structured process for investigating a network phenomenon in a data-driven manner (Huhtamäki et al. 2015). The Model was developed through several rounds of Action Design Research (ADR) taking place at different levels of abstraction and complexity in innovation ecosystems. The Model allows taking a visual analytics approach to investigate innovation ecosystems through networks using a computational data-driven method. It builds on several streams of literature on information visualization (Card et al. 1999), data-driven visualization pipelines (Nykänen et al. 2008), visual analytics (Wong and Thomas 2004), interactive visual analysis (Heer and Shneiderman 2012) and visual network analysis (Freeman 2000). The Model combines and extends several process models including the information visualization reference model, the visual analytics model (Keim et al. 2010), and most importantly the Network Analysis and Visualization (NAV) process model (Hansen et al. 2012).

Our overall perspective embodied by the Ostinato Model is in sync with Bendoly (2016). We affirm that visualization is of utmost utility in supporting the full investigative process from validation of data sources and feedback mechanism for data cleaning and aggregation, through exploration and discovery, to sharing the findings with others in a way that allows them to contextualize according to their worldviews, articulate their biases and conduct group-level sensemaking.

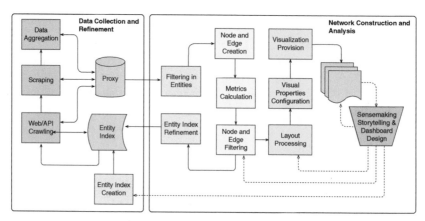

FIGURE 5.1 Ostinato Model for Visual Network Analytics

Source: Adapted from Huhtamäki et al. 2015

Key principles of the Ostinato Model are transparency, continuous data collection, exploration, loose coupling, interoperability, reproducibility, automation, enabling manual steps and low entry barrier. The Model has two phases: Data Collection and Refinement; and Network Creation and Analysis. The Data Collection and Refinement phase is further divided into Entity Index Creation, Web/API Crawling, Scraping and Data Aggregation. The Network Construction and Analysis phase is composed of Filtering in Entities, Node and Edge Creation, Metrics Calculation, Node and Edge Filtering, Entity Index Refinement, Layout Processing and Visual Properties Configuration (see Figure 5.1). A cycle of exploration and automation characterizes the Model and is embedded in each phase.

Another key principle of the Ostinato Model is enabling process transparency and easy access for all members of an interdisciplinary team to data (e.g. tabular representation) in all possible phases of the analytical process. The use of standard data-processing tools is recommended, including spreadsheet processors for accessing the data as it prioritizes implementing many types of diagnostic and explorative analyses to support the collaborative sensemaking processes of multiple investigators as co-creators of insights.

5.2 Appreciating the Audience and Context

Innovation ecosystems are open and, more specifically, complex adaptive systems (Thomas and Autio 2012). These properties yield analytic requirements that are very difficult to measure and benchmark. To operate in this complex domain, we subscribe to Critical Realist philosophy to establish an epistemological and ontological platform for the investigations, and we agree with Dobson (2001) in acknowledging the importance of taking a philosophical stance in establishing a common platform for investigative work. In short, Critical Realist research combines realist ontology with interpretive epistemology (Bygstad and Munkvold 2011). This assumes that generalizable structures and mechanisms exist in social phenomenon. In order to identify these mechanisms and structures, however, investigators must move beyond superficial statistical measurements and case-specific qualitative observations to apply several complementing methods, both qualitative and quantitative, in the investigations. More pragmatically, we point to Bygstad and Munkvold (2011) who introduce Critical Realism as an approach to data analytics and claim that analytics processes should serve the objective of identifying the structures and mechanisms that exist within phenomenon and surface as observable events. We further agree with Dobson (2001) and Archer (1995) that social structure should be observed as dynamic, and therefore, that studying its evolution over time is important, that social structure is both a key driver of social activity, and that social activity is a key driver of the evolution of social structure.

Further, to contribute to the body of knowledge in visual analytics of innovation ecosystems, and more specifically to dig deeper into the data-processing requirements for the Ostinato Model, we take an ADR approach (Sein et al. 2011) to develop new analytics IT and information artifacts that support the investigative processes of the innovation ecosystems. In ADR, artifact development takes place in between researchers and the organization to whose requirements the artifacts are developed to satisfy. Guided emergence is the core process of ADR, i.e. the artifact emerges through intensive interaction rather than being developed first and then evaluated. Guided emergence takes place in Build–Intervene–Evaluate (BIE) cycles, in which concurrent evaluation is an organic part (Sein et al. 2011).

One focal application context for our approach has been EIT ICT Labs, currently operating as EIT Digital,"a leading European open innovation organisation" (www.eitdigital.eu/about-us/overview/). We joined with EIT ICT Labs management in the beginning of their operation to investigate the existing connections between the then six co-location cities (Still et al. 2014) and again after several years of activities has transpired. The Innovation Ecosystems Network Dataset (IEND), a socially constructed set of data on growth companies, their key individuals and investors, was used to as the sole source of data (Rubens et al. 2010).

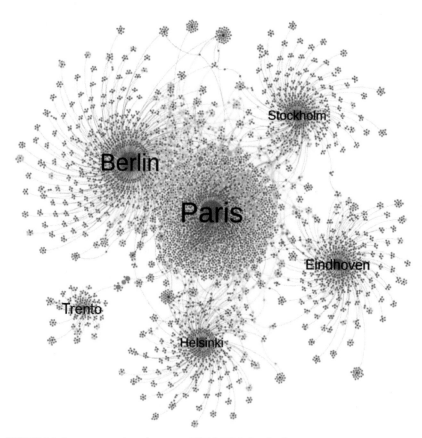

FIGURE 5.2 Interconnections between EIT ICT Labs Co-locations

Source: Adapted from Still et al. 2014

In network visualization in Figure 5.2, the EIT ICT Labs co-location cities are represented as nodes and connected to all companies having their main office in that city. The companies are further connected to each key individual in the dataset with whom they are or have been affiliated. Moreover, the companies are connected to their investors. Acquisitions form connections between individual companies. Betweenness centrality is used to size the nodes in the visualization, and nodes are laid out with Force Atlas 2 (Bastian et al. 2009). Figure 5.3 shows the Ostinato Model variation for the EIT ICT Labs investigation.

Using betweenness centrality as the key metric and force-driven algorithm for laying out the nodes, we were able to highlight the nodes that showed mobility in between the co-location centers. The key connecting tissue between the co-location centers was further highlighted through filtering in nodes according to their betweenness centrality value. Two key insights were achieved through the investigation. First, investors emerged as the key source of mobility in the existing EIT ICT Labs innovation ecosystem and, therefore, ways to engage the investors close to EIT ICT Labs operations needed to be investigated. Second, on the basis of the visualization of the inclusion of the San Francisco Bay Area as the then hypothetical seventh node of EIT ICT Labs in Figure 5.4, it was argued that the Bay Area could be, in fact, the most important connector among the six European cities in which EIT ICT Labs was operating at the time.

In another example, several different datasets were federated to provide a multidimensional perspective. Investigation of the Finnish Innovation Ecosystem using three different datasets in parallel and as a federated dataset added complexity to the data processing of the Ostinato Model (Still et al. 2013). Each of the three datasets—Thomson Reuters SDC, IEND Executives and Finance, and IEND Angels and Startups—addressed a different part of the innovation ecosystem, yet with some overlap. To allow for international comparability, we chose not to include data on the funding that many of the Finnish companies had received from Finnish Funding Agency for Innovation Tekes, a governmental agency that

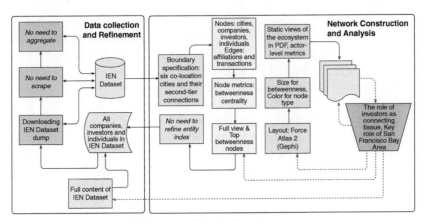

FIGURE 5.3 Ostinato Model for EIT ICT Labs Investigation

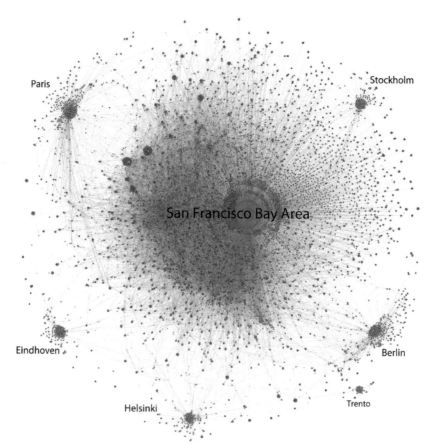

FIGURE 5.4 What if San Francisco Bay Area Would Be the Seventh City?

Source: Adapted from Still et al. 2014

supports a significant portion of Research and Development in Finnish companies. The Ostinato Model variation in Figure 5.5 shows the process applied in
the Finnish Innovation Ecosystem investigation. A separate data collection and
refinement process was used (marked as a deck of three distinct processes) for each
dataset. Moreover, the network representations were also created through separate
processes. Analysis using an aggregation of the datasets was conducted only after
the network representations had been constructed and validated.

The resulting multiscopic views allowed for a number of confirmatory and
novel insights on the Finnish innovation ecosystem. Nokia's role was visible in all
the different ecosystem viewpoints. A handful of key individuals played integral
roles, and a key source of venture capital consisted of government-based organizations. Student-based Startup Sauna, a non-institutional entity, also had a prominent role as a source of new activity.

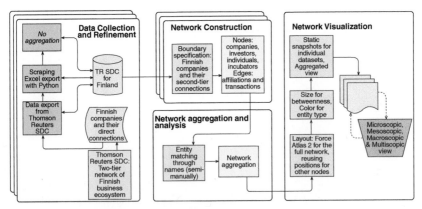

FIGURE 5.5 Ostinato Model for Finnish Innovation Ecosystem Investigation

5.3   Design Principles Applied

The innovation ecosystem investigations we have conducted, including the two examples described in the previous section, have required making a number of design decisions related to collecting and processing the transactional microdata, from its original form to network representations. In this section, we describe and discuss a number of data-processing related design decisions and their impact on the investigative process. For tractability, we pin the issues to the various phases of the Ostinato Model. The design issues and related steps of the Ostinato Model are included in Table 5.1.

Boundary Specification

There are several ways that investigative teams can specify the boundaries of the innovation ecosystem under investigation (cf. Basole et al. 2012). Boundary specification indirectly impacts all the different phases of the investigative process. Importantly, the investigators should be able to experiment with various options for the boundaries to better understand their effects. Moreover, we note that in country-level investigations we have chosen to follow the national boundaries in a fashion similar to more traditional ways of measuring innovation—through survey data—while the computational approach comes with reduced workload for crossing the boundaries.

Source Data Format

Useful data sources for innovation ecosystem investigations are available in various formats from websites that require crawling and scraping to machine-readable spreadsheets ready to be used for computational analysis. This chapter does not cover the wide variety of practices for data access that are available. It is, however, worth mentioning that in most investigations we have relied on using MongoDB

TABLE 5.1 Data-processing Related Design Issues and Their Use in Ostinato Model Phases

Design Issue	Data Collection and Refinement	Network Construction and Analysis
Boundary specification	Entity Index Creation	Entity Index Refinement
Source data format	All phases	
Tabular data representation	Scraping, Data Aggregation	Node and Edge Creation Metrics Calculation, Note and Edge Filtering
Temporal data		Filtering in entities, Note and Edge Filtering, Visualization Provision
Graph-based filtering		Filtering in entities, Node and Edge Filtering
Volumetrically big data	All phases	Entity Index Refinement, Metrics Calculation, Visualization Provision
Multiple data sources	Data Aggregation	
Ability to filter		Node and Edge Creation, Node and Edge Filtering
One-mode or multimode networks		Node and Edge Creation, Metrics Calculation

as a means for implementing a data proxy. Key virtues of MongoDB, a NoSQL database, are the flexibility of the data schema and ability to search the data.

Tabular Data Representation

A key principle for enabling process transparency and easy access to all members of the interdisciplinary team is using tabular data representation in all possible phases of the process. Importantly, this allows the use of standard data-processing tools, including spreadsheet processors for accessing the data, and implementing the kinds of diagnostic and explorative analysis that support investigators' sensemaking processes. While this observation or principle may seem obvious, we would like to point out the plethora of options that a skilled data scientist has available for managing the data from NoSQL and relational databases to graph databases and big data technologies, including Apache Hadoop and Spark.

Temporal Data is Imperative

We do want to stress the importance of the availability of transactional microdata on innovation ecosystem actors. With transactional microdata, we refer to data that includes timestamps of the activities taking place in between explicitly identified innovation ecosystem actors. Examples of activities include individuals founding a startup, a serial entrepreneur joining the board, startups raising a round of venture capital from specified angel and organizational investors, firms acquiring a startup, and firms announcing an Initial Public Offering in a specified stock exchange.

Graph-based Filtering

A major exception to the default rule for representing data in tabular format is cases in which boundary specification is being conducted with k-step rules (Basole et al. 2012), i.e. rules that: i) specify inclusion filter for a set of nodes; and ii) further include nodes that are k-steps away from the included nodes. While we have so far implemented this part of the analysis pipeline by crawling entities on the basis of recursive inclusion rules, we point to practices available in graph databases—the likes of Cypher for Neo4j and SparQL for Resource Description Framework—to specify filtering rules based on network topology. Also, self-service tools such as Gephi implement topology-based filters that allow expressing simple boundary specification rules.

Volumetrically Big Data

Data that is truly big in volume does require special arrangements for its management. Additionally, a key restriction in visual network analysis is, however, the amount of pixels available for provisioning the network visualization. According to our experience, a manageable network size for visual analytics is in the scale of thousands or tens of thousands of nodes. From a technical viewpoint it is important to note that the limit of data becoming big in volume depends heavily on the selection of analytical technology, including spreadsheet processors and other stock tools for exploration used by the investigators.

Multiple Data Sources

In the investigation of the Finnish Innovation Ecosystem (Still et al. 2013) we used complementing sets of data—both in parallel and, importantly, as an aggregate—to create a multiscopic view of the innovation ecosystem. To create the multiscopic view, we first created dataset-specific representations of the innovation ecosystem. The aggregate set of data was then composed through a process of finding the entities—in this investigation companies, investors, and individuals—that appeared in more than one dataset and creating a unique identifier for each, which was used across the datasets. We used a semi-manual process to create the identifiers for this particular investigation.

The use of multiple sets of data in parallel is for us the key venue for future development. At best, the datasets are aggregated as the very first step of the analysis process. This allows for boundary specification in a consistent way that takes into account cross-dataset connections between entities. Aggregating full sets of volumetric data, however, insists on full automation of the process. Approaches for achieving this call for applying machine learning techniques from string matching (Navarro 2001) to named entity recognition (Finkel et al. 2005).

Balancing between Aggregation and Expressivity for Filtering

The mantra "system visualizations require systems of visuals" introduced in Chapter 1 applies fully to the domain of innovation ecosystem analytics. To support decision making among individuals with divergent perspectives and objectives, the visualizations can facilitate the development of a shared vision (Russell et al. 2015), which provides an "intelligent fit" and guides decisions.

Processing data for a static snapshot representation of innovation ecosystem structure, i.e. for a static picture, introduces requirements that are completely different from those of creating a network representation that allows for interactive exploration—important in discovering the "intelligent fit"—and analysis of the innovation ecosystem. While both snapshot and interactive approaches are specific to downstream tools in the analysis process, this is particularly the case for interactive analytics. Importantly, from the information visualization process model to visual analytics principles, we stressed the importance permitting the visualization users to interact with all the different phases of the process from data collection to cleaning to transformation to analysis and visualization.

One-mode or Multi-mode Networks

Across a wide spectrum of innovation ecosystem visual representations, ranging from a local innovation ecosystem engager Demola Tampere (Huhtamäki et al. 2013), to continent-wide, global-reaching EIT ICT Labs, we have designed one-mode and multi-mode networks. Some of the design processes were implemented within the research team per se, and in others, additional innovation ecosystem actors joined the design process. For reasons of data availability and application objectives, we have usually relied on multi-mode networks to represent innovation ecosystem structures. From a quantitative network analysis viewpoint, this is not optimal; one-mode directed networks would allow us to use the widest possible set of node-level metrics for identifying actors' structural roles. However, one-mode representation requires reducing the complexity of the innovation ecosystem; consequently, this leads to a heightened need for investigators' awareness and understanding of the data processing done "under the hood"—more sophistication demanded for "intelligent fit."

In addition to the design issues described above, we have identified a set of overarching themes that should be considered as part of the design rationale of the data-processing architecture. These include decisions on the extent to which the organic complexity of the innovation ecosystem should be reduced, the data-sourcing approach between in-house and external data, and the use of graph-based data-management practices throughout the data-processing architecture.

Complexity Versus Clarity

Out of the four categories of Cynefin model—simple, complicated, complex and chaotic (Snowden and Boone 2007)—innovation ecosystems are either complex or chaotic. This complexity further highlights the importance to take into account the biases of human cognition discussed in Chapter 1. We claim that this nature of the phenomenon should be visible in its visual representation especially when a newly composed team investigates a previously unexplored innovation ecosystem. In other words, more specific representations are needed in subsequent steps—to drill down (See section 2.3 in Chapter 2) into the ways that individual mechanisms contribute to system-level behavior. Our experience shows that innovation ecosystem actors representing governmental organizations and early-phase start-ups often share very little in their worldviews. We believe that aligning divergent worldviews, by discussing the structure and mechanisms underlying an innovation ecosystem, is imperative. We look forward to future investigations to explore the process of enacted sensemaking (Weick et al. 2005) as detailed in section 3.3, in Chapter 3.

From In-house to External Data

When building up their operations, EIT ICT Labs invited us to join with them in developing a visual analytics artifact to support their work in exploring the existing interconnection between, at the time, six co-location centers. We started the exploration with internal data collected to represent their engineered activities. Together, we soon learned to realize that the insights afforded by this data were in most cases already known to the EIT ICT Labs orchestrators. Therefore, we chose to source data for analytics from another source—the IEN Dataset, as mentioned before.

5.4   Lessons for Future Development

Why not use graph representation from the beginning of the process, then? This approach is indeed worth considering. A few observations are in order, however.

First, should graph representation of the source data be used, all members of the investigative team need to be able to access the data through an interactive exploratory user interface, perhaps operated with a web browser. Second, it should be possible to export full sets of source data, both actor and transaction data, in tabular format for further investigations with spreadsheet processors and other self-service analytics tools. Third, it is important to realize that building a graph database with the data collected from various sources is effectively the process of building a network representation of the innovation ecosystem, an iterative development process for which the Ostinato Model can be used.

Another major improvement to add expressivity to the analytics process would be creating network-shaped projections of network data through queries and filters that are based on combinations of network topology and properties of actors and transactions. This capability would greatly benefit the creation of different views of full network representations of innovation ecosystems. For example, through network representation of the existing six co-location centers and related actors in the EIT ICT Labs ecosystem, we visually observed that Paris and Berlin are close to each other in terms of network topology. The green belt between the two cities suggests that a large number of investors operate in the two cities adding to their interconnectedness. When San Francisco Bay Area is added as the seventh EIT Digital node, however, the relative interconnectedness of Berlin and Paris became less significant than the interconnectedness of the Bay Area. Alternative explanations were possible. To explore whether this was due to the fact that the investors in the first visualization were largely also operating in the San Francisco Bay Area would require filtering the data. An expressive way to do this could be to use filters that are based on network topology and properties of actors and their interconnections.

We foresee two key streams of future work. The Ostinato Model provides a firm platform for further innovation ecosystem investigations conducted using a data-driven visual network analytics approach; we have a firm basis for future investigations. This allows continued experiments with the ADR approach and Critical Realist mindset. We want to echo Freeman's (2000) call for further work in developing infrastructure for visual network analysis—i.e. to develop systems of visual for system visualization (Chapter 1): "We can look forward to similar progress in developing database programs designed to facilitate the storage and retrieval of social network data. But the real breakthrough will occur when we develop a single program that can integrate these three kinds of tools into a single program." While easy-access tools such as NodeXL and commercial tools including Palantir and Quid are available, a major need exists for component-based lightweight analysis processes that allow for data-driven visual network analytics investigations in the context of business and innovation ecosystems and beyond.

Second, at a more conceptual level, we encourage an analysis of the data-driven visual network analytics process to identify and describe in detail the three subsystems within the overall Information System artifact: i) technological artifact, ii) information artifact and iii) social artifact (Lee et al. 2015). We expect that this analysis will allow for further specificity in future rounds of ADR, in which new artifacts for innovation ecosystem visual analytics are created through guided emergence. We are thrilled to observe the development steps that the editors, authors and readers of the book at hand will make in developing new systems of visuals to support collaborative visual analytics and visualization-supported enacted sensemaking in organizations.

References

Adner, Ron, and Rahul Kapoor. 2010. "Value Creation in Innovation Ecosystems: How the Structure of Technological Interdependence Affects Firm Performance in New Technology Generations." *Strategic Management Journal* 31 (3) (March): 306–333. doi:10.1002/smj.821.

Archer, Margaret S. 1995. *Realist Social Theory: The Morphogenetic Approach*. Cambridge, MA: Cambridge University Press.

Basole, Rahul C., Martha G. Russell, Jukka Huhtamäki, and Neil Rubens. 2012. "Understanding Mobile Ecosystem Dynamics: A Data-Driven Approach." In *Proceedings of the 2012 International Conference on Mobile Business (ICMB 2012)*, 17–28.

Bastian, Mathieu, Sebastien Heymann, and Mathieu Jacomy. 2009. "Gephi: An Open Source Software for Exploring and Manipulating Networks." In *Proceedings of the Third International AAAI Conference on Weblogs and Social Media, May 17–20, 2009, San Jose, California, USA*.

Bendoly, Elliot. 2016. "Fit, Bias and Enacted Sensemaking in Data Visualization: Frameworks for Continuous in Operations and Supply Chain Management Analytics." *Journal of Business Logistics*.

Bygstad, Bendik, and Bjørn Erik Munkvold. 2011. "In Search of Mechanisms. Conducting a Critical Realist Data Analysis." In 32nd *International Conference on Information Systems, Shanghai 2011*.

Card, Stuart, Jock Mackinlay, and Ben Shneiderman. 1999. *Readings in Information Visualization: Using Vision to Think*. 1st ed. San Francisco, CA: Morgan Kaufmann.

Dobson, Philip J. 2001. "The Philosophy of Critical Realism—An Opportunity for Information Systems Research." *Information Systems Frontiers* 3 (2) (June): 199–210. doi:10.1023/A:1011495424958.

Finkel, Jenny Rose, Trond Grenager, and Christopher Manning. 2005. "Incorporating Non-Local Information into Information Extraction Systems by Gibbs Sampling." In *ACL '05*. Stroudsburg, PA, USA: Association for Computational Linguistics, 363–370. doi:10.3115/1219840.1219885.

Freeman, Linton C. 2000. "Visualizing Social Networks." *Journal of Social Structure* 1 (1): [np]. www.cmu.edu/joss/content/articles/volume1/Freeman.html [accessed November 27, 2015].

Hansen, Derek L., Dana Rotman, Elizabeth Bonsignore, Nataa Milic-Frayling, Eduarda Mendes Rodrigues, Marc Smith, and Ben Shneiderman. 2012. "Do You Know the Way to SNA?: A Process Model for Analyzing and Visualizing Social Media Network Data." In *Proceedings of the 2012 International Conference on Social Informatics*, IEEE. 304–313. doi:10.1109/SocialInformatics.2012.26 [accessed January 15, 2016].

Heer, Jeffrey, and Ben Shneiderman. 2012. "Interactive Dynamics for Visual Analysis." *Communications of the ACM* 55 (4): 45–54.

Huhtamäki, Jukka, Ville Luotonen, Ville Kairamo, Kaisa Still, and Martha G. Russell. 2013. "Process for Measuring and Visualizing an Open Innovation Platform: Case Demola." In *17th International Academic Mind Trek Conference 2013: "Making Sense of Converging Media,"* *October 1–3, Tampere, Finland*. ACM. http://urn.fi/URN:NBN:fi:tty-201312201533 [accessed January 7, 2015].

Huhtamäki, Jukka, Martha G. Russell, Neil Rubens, and Kaisa Still. 2015. "Ostinato: The Exploration-Automation Cycle of User-Centric, Process-Automated Data-Driven Visual Network Analytics." In *Transparency in Social Media: Tools, Methods and Algorithms for Mediating Online Interactions*, edited by Sorin Adam Matei, Martha G. Russell, and Elisa

Bertino, 197–222. Switzerland: Springer International Publishing Switzerland. http://link.springer.com/chapter/10.1007/978-3-319-18552-1_11 [accessed December 17, 2015].

Huhtamäki, Jukka, Martha G. Russell, Kaisa Still, and Neil Rubens. 2011. "A Network-Centric Snapshot of Value Co-Creation in Finnish Innovation Financing." *Open Source Business Resource* (March): 13–21. www.osbr.ca/ojs/index.php/osbr/article/view/1288/1234.

Hwang, Victor W., and Greg Horowitt. 2012. *The Rainforest: The Secret to Building the Next Silicon Valley*. 1.02 ed. Los Altos Hills, CA: Regenwald.

Iansiti, Marco, and Roy Levien. 2004. *The Keystone Advantage: What the New Dynamics of Business Ecosystems Mean for Strategy, Innovation, and Sustainability*. Boston, MA: Harvard Business Review Press.

Järvi, Kati, and Samuli Kortelainen. 2016. "Taking Stock of Empirical Research on Business Ecosystems: A Literature Review." *International Journal of Business and Systems Research*: Forthcoming.

Keim, Daniel, Jörn Kohlhammer, Geoffrey Ellis, and Florian Mansmann. 2010. *Mastering the Information Age - Solving Problems with Visual Analytics*. Eurographics Association. www.vismaster.eu/book/ [accessed December 17, 2015].

Lee, Allen S., Manoj Thomas, and Richard L. Baskerville. 2015. "Going Back to Basics in Design Science: From the Information Technology Artifact to the Information Systems Artifact." *Information Systems Journal* 25 (1) (January): 5–21. doi:10.1111/isj.12054.

Moore, James F. 1993. "Predators and Prey: A New Ecology of Competition." *Harvard Business Review* 71 (3): 75–86.

Navarro, Gonzalo. 2001. "A Guided Tour to Approximate String Matching." *ACM Comput. Surv.* 33 (1) (March): 31–88. doi:10.1145/375360.375365.

Nykänen, Ossi, Jaakko Salonen, Matti Haapaniemi, and Jukka Huhtamäki. 2008. "A Visualisation System for a Peer-to-Peer Information Space." In *Proceedings of the 2nd International OPAALs Conference on Digital Ecosystems*, 76–85. Tampere, Finland: Tampere University of Technology.

Pentland, Alex "Sandy." 2015. *Social Physics: How Social Networks Can Make Us Smarter*. New York, NY: Penguin Books.

Ramaswamy, Venkat. 2009. "Leading the Transformation to Co-creation of Value." *Strategy & Leadership* 37 (2) (March): 32–37. doi:10.1108/10878570910941208. www.emeraldinsight.com/doi/abs/10.1108/10878570910941208.

Ritala, Paavo, and Pia Hurmelinna-Laukkanen. 2009. "What's in It for Me? Creating and Appropriating Value in Innovation-Related Coopetition." *Technovation* 29 (12) (December): 819–828. doi:10.1016/j.technovation.2009.07.002.

Rubens, Neil, Kaisa Still, Jukka Huhtamäki, and Martha G. Russell. 2010. "Leveraging Social Media for Analysis of Innovation Players and Their Moves." Innovation Ecosystems Consortium.

Russell, Martha G., Jukka Huhtamäki, Kaisa Still, Neil Rubens, and Rahul C. Basole. 2015. "Relational Capital for Shared Vision in Innovation Ecosystems." *Triple Helix: A Journal of University-Industry-Government Innovation and Entrepreneurship (THJI)*.

Russell, Martha G., Kaisa Still, Jukka Huhtamäki, Camilla Yu, and Neil Rubens. 2011. "Transforming Innovation Ecosystems through Shared Vision and Network Orchestration." In Stanford, CA, USA. *Triple Helix IX International Conference: Silicon Valley: Global Model or Unique Anomaly?, At Stanford, California, USA*.

Sein, Maung, Ola Henfridsson, Sandeep Purao, Matti Rossi, and Rikard Lindgren. 2011. "Action Design Research." *MIS Quarterly* 35 (1): 37–56.

Snowden, David J., and Mary E. Boone. 2007. "A Leader's Framework for Decision Making." November.

Still, Kaisa, Jukka Huhtamäki, Martha G. Russell, Rahul C. Basole, Jaakko Salonen, and Neil Rubens. 2013. "Networks of Innovation Relationships: Multiscopic Views on Finland." In *Proceedings of the XXIV ISPIM Conference—Innovating in Global Markets: Challenges for Sustainable Growth, 161–9 June 2013, Helsinki, Finland*, 15.

Still, Kaisa, Jukka Huhtamäki, Martha G. Russell, and Neil Rubens. 2012. "Paradigm Shift in Innovation Indicators: From Analog to Digital." In *Proceedings of the 5th ISPIM Innovation Forum, 91–2 December, 2012, Seoul, Korea*.

Still, Kaisa, Jukka Huhtamäki, Martha G. Russell, and Neil Rubens. 2014. "Insights for Orchestrating Innovation Ecosystems: The Case of EIT ICT Labs and Data-Driven Network Visualisations." *International Journal of Technology Management* 66 (2/3) (January): 243–265. doi:10.1504/IJTM.2014.064606. www.inderscienceonline.com/doi/abs/10.1504/IJTM.2014.064606.

Thomas, Llewellyn D.W., and Erkko Autio. 2012. "Modeling the Ecosystem: A Meta-Synthesis of Ecosystem and Related Literatures." In *DRUID 2012, June 19–21, CBS, Copenhagen, Denmark.*, 28.

Weick, Karl E., Kathleen M. Sutcliffe, and David Obstfeld. 2005. "Organizing and the Process of Sensemaking." *Organization Science* 16 (4) (August): 409–421. doi:10.1287/orsc.1050.0133.

Wong, Pak Chung, and J. Thomas. 2004. "Visual Analytics." *IEEE Computer Graphics and Applications* 24 (5) (October): 20–21. doi:10.1109/MCG.2004.39. http://ieeexplore.ieee.org/ielx5/38/29442/01333623.pdf?tp=&arnumber=1333623&isnumber=29442.

PART II
Applied Cases

6

VISUALIZING A REAL-WORLD SALES PIPELINE PROCESS

Jeremy C. Adams

In most business settings data visualization can be used to communicate a story that incentivizes desired behavior. Techniques from behavioral operations, behavioral economics and human perception analysis can be put to use with data visualizations to tell that story. The following hypothetical scenario is based upon the author's real-world experiences in a variety of business settings. In this scenario a small sales organization has been using a new software tool to grow sales revenues, improve sales contract profitability and to improve customer service outcomes. In this story we will see both good and bad examples of data visualization, behaviors that are driven by the visualizations used, and data visualization enhancements that improved the perceptions and behaviors of those consuming the information.

The year is 2012, and Acme Medical has been growing their medical rehabilitation equipment business in the long-term care marketplace for the past two years with limited success. The company knows they are ten years behind their biggest competitors in this growing marketplace. However, they also know that they need to become a competitive supplier of products to long-term care facilities in order to remain a strong medical equipment manufacturer. Acme Medical's two small sales teams, divided by east and west regions, service the entire US market of long-term care facilities. Additionally, a single call center provides 24-hour support for some of Acme Medical's more advanced products such as elliptical machines, treadmills and stationary bikes.

Acme has just completed a project to build a new software system that provides the sales and customer service staff with access to an advanced series of pricing and customer demographic information that is unlike any other tool available to Acme's competitors. This tool replaces several manual processes for both sales teams and the customer service team, but also requires new workflow processes to be followed by these teams.

Pricing and IT managers want full adoption of the new technology to grow revenues, increase profit margins, improve customer support services and reduce the time to approve new customer contracts. However, adoption by sales staff is expected to be difficult since the sales team has little time to work on a computer while connected to Acme's internal network. Additionally, the customer service staff still thinks some of their manual processes will provide a better customer experience than using the new system will. It is a common phenomenon of new system implementations to experience these types of reactions from employees (cf. Bendoly and Cotteleer 2008, Cotteleer and Bendoly 2006). Acme knew it would be necessary to incentivize change in this instance as well.

In order to incentivize both teams to use the new system, the sales team has been given a 100 percent utilization "objective"—involving the use of the tool for all new customer deals as part of their year-end goals. The customer service team has been given a small quarterly income bonus incentive for a 90 percent utilization rate on all customer calls. The IT and pricing managers ask their lead business consultant to develop a series of weekly and monthly reports about the new tool. The two core questions to be answered are as follows: How good is the tool at improving the sales lifecycle pipeline? How well are the customer service and sales staff performing against stated goals of using the new system?

6.1 Appreciating the Audience and Context

The lead business consultant now has a difficult job. Answering any one of the questions posed by IT and pricing managers will require more than one way of reviewing the data. The first question, "How good is the tool at improving the sales lifecycle pipeline?" is vague and unspecific. What is the definition of "good"? How do we define "improving"? Can we fully measure the cost-benefit of all given states in the sales lifecycle pipeline? Rather than become stuck attempting to answer these questions through competing and contradictory opinions by management, the consultant decides to present some initial data to gain feedback on how to proceed with better visualizations. To begin, the consultant retrieves data about all of the customers entered into the new tool, and prepares a simple cross-reference count of the data. The cross-reference data is embodied by the Table 6.1 example.

TABLE 6.1 End of Month Customer Deal Status

	FY2012	End of Month Customer Deal Status											
	Current	Jul	Aug	Sep	Oct	Nov	Dec	Jan	Feb	Mar	Apr	May	Jun
# of Customers	165	22	43	56	81	92	96	111	121	124	138	144	165
Sales Pipeline Status													
Work in Progress	125	22	57	77	85	99	90	54	61	69	82	90	125
Pending	22	9	7	5	3	11	4	12	7	8	15	19	22
Approved	101	3	15	35	49	65	66	57	40	57	69	77	101
Rejected	30	1	9	9	11	16	18	17	20	12	25	33	30
Accepted	44	1	4	2	0	6	12	3	3	2	0	5	6
Declined	37	1	3	1	2	0	2	7	10	2	2	6	1

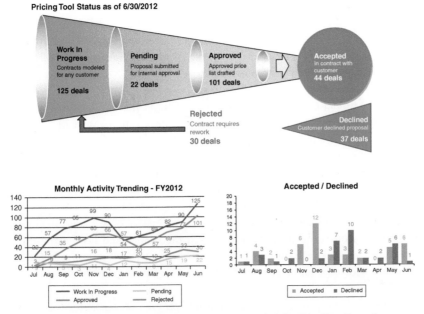

FIGURE 6.1 Graphical Visualization of Data Points with Sales Pipeline Funnel

The pricing manager likes the information, but feels that a graphical data visualization would help contextualize the various states that a deal goes through before being accepted or declined by the customer. The manager provides a template from a prior project, and asks the consultant to keep it updated with the previous month's data so that it can be presented each month to both technical and non-technical senior managers. The consultant prepares the following slide, as captured in Figure 6.1.

The pricing manager is pleased with this view of data, and believes that it tells a positive story about the use of the tool. While the information presented in Table 6.1 and Figure 6.1 use exactly the same data, the graphical visualization of Figure 6.1 tells a different story than does the raw data presentation of Table 6.1. Initial assumptions by top leadership predicted no more than 50 deals in the pipeline at any one time, associated specifically with tool use. They further anticipated that only ten contracts would be closed by the end of the fiscal year. According to this visualization, the tool has been a resounding success with 44 total accepted contracts and 37 rejected contracts, and a large volume of contracts in the sales pipeline. Top leadership decides to increase the budget of the IT and pricing manager's teams to continue to support and improve the new tool.

6.2 Design Principles Applied

But why did senior managers arrive at these conclusions? More critically, were these appropriate conclusions to make given the data presented?

In fact, these were not correct conclusions to make. Pay careful attention to the sales pipeline funnel shown in Figure 6.1. Using a funnel to represent components of the sales process is not a new concept, and doing so can be traced back to 1898 when E. St. Elmo Lewis first articulated the Awareness–Interest–Desire–Action sales motivation model (discussed in Friedman 1998). However, the funnel shown in Figure 6.1 documents a different process.

First, the funnel of Figure 6.1 obscures facts about the process that could be reasonably observed by studying the numeric values in the context of what the process actually is. For instance, notice the total area decreasing with each subsequent phase of the funnel, and how the area of each phase is not representative of the numeric values shown. Also notice how the stages of the funnel are a mixture of internal processes (Pending/Approved) and customer motivation factors (Accepted/Declined).

Second, if we follow the flow depicted it is unclear how many previously Rejected deals have been sent back through the funnel, and how many times they have been sent back through. The Declined arrow that is pointing to the left with same red color as the Rejected arrow can be perceived as a non-final state for any given deal.

In this case, the pricing manager's reliance on existing templates that told a positive story in a previous context do not correctly represent the story or context of the data in question (see associated discussions in Chapter 2). Another interpretation of the pricing manager's motivation could be that using the existing template to intentionally obscure some of the details of the process was useful to encourage full 100 percent adoption of the tool by the sales staff. In any case, this template was a singular point of reference to the data, and a better means of visualizing the data could be implemented.

Fortunately, the consultant in this case noticed the biases invoked and heuristics adopted by senior management when reviewing Figure 6.1, and decided to redesign the visualization to provide a clearer representation for both internal processes and customer decision-making. Figure 6.2, the revised report that the consultant prepared, more accurately depicts the context of both aspects of the sales process across time—internal workflow processes and external customer decisions.

Now the data tells a far different story about the new pricing tool. First, we can see that the ratio of Work in Progress to Approved deals is about the same within the first three to four months of the implementation of the new pricing tool. Second, the decline in the average number of times a deal was rejected over the first year can be seen to be potentially inversely correlated to the increase in the Cumulative Win Ratio. This new system of visualizations allowed senior managers to identify several new questions to be answered: Is the finance team moving deals through the "Pending" stage faster than necessary? Even though the average number of rejections per deal continues to decline, indicating better pricing structure of each new deal, the Cumulative Win Ratio appears to be stuck

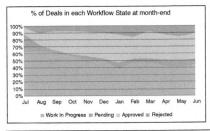

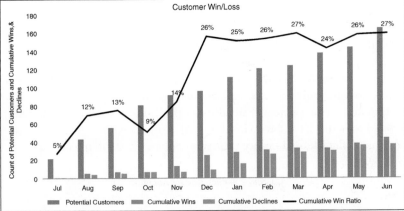

FIGURE 6.2 A Revised View of the Sales Pipeline Activity Data

at 26 percent. Are we leaving money on the table by being too aggressive with our current pricing strategies? Since December the ratio of won vs. lost deals has plateaued at 26 percent—is that ratio better or worse than our competitors?

We see that the consultant's use of ratios combined with the time dimension in each case improves interpretability of the data, and unveils trends occurring within the sales lifecycle that managers need to be aware of in order to improve outcomes. The breakdown of the data into more discrete components in the form of separate charts also helps focus the viewer, and leads managers to identify previously unnoticed concerns. In doing so, the system of idioms developed provides a much stronger fit to the actual needs for system-wide comprehension—hence coinciding with the recommendations made in Chapter 3.

6.3 Examination of Use

The next series of visualizations that the consultant was tasked with building were reports tracking the adoption for both the sales team and customer service teams. The consultant decided to provide two separate visualizations of their activity. The first stacked area chart provided a view of the customer service team's gradual but consistent adoption of using old customer contact management methods even while contact volumes more than doubled during the year.

An interview with the customer service manager highlighted how valuable the new tool had been in allowing the customer service teams to handle the drastic increase in contacts, and in how much happier customers were with the faster resolution of issues since the adoption of the new tool. The consultant highlighted this fact by annotating the first chart as can be seen in Figure 6.3. Rather than placing the percent of contacts handled using the new process in a separate chart, the consultant decided to annotate the call volumes with the ratio since the loss of the "red" area in the chart over time indicated the overall adoption was strong for the customer service teams.

As in Figure 6.3, Figure 6.4 was intended to show the difference in adoption of the new tool by the sales team, but rather than change the style of chart the consultant decided to use the same stacked area chart.

The consultant felt that this series of visualizations appropriately conveyed the right message to both audiences. Unfortunately, on initial design, the consultant did not take into account potential Trend Biases that led to the following interpretation of these charts (as discussed in Chapter 1). In this case, when these charts were presented to the sales and finance managers both managers interpreted that system

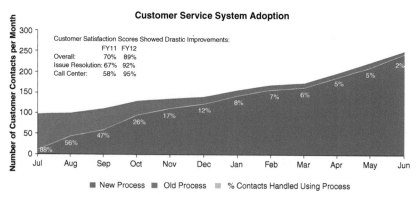

FIGURE 6.3 Customer Service System Adoption Stacked Area Chart

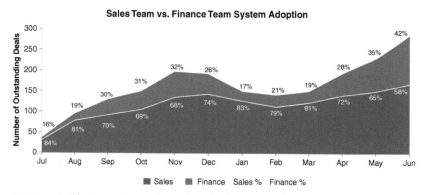

FIGURE 6.4 Sales Team System Adoption Stacked Area Chart

adoption was increasing for the sales team as well. The consultant explained that the percentages showed a negative trend. The sales and finance managers then understood the way the numbers were being presented, and they then suggested a new method be developed to show this relationship more clearly to senior managers.

The fact that the consultant had to go through this process of explanation threw him off guard. Were both managers not reading the percentages on the chart? Did they not see the divergence of the red portion of the stacked area chart in the last few months of the year? What actually triggered the particular form of Trend Bias that seems to take place (when other trend interpretations were also viable)?

In reality the trigger that routed interpretation was likely a simple but often surprising aspect of human perception: Availability Bias (Chapters 1 and 2). In the situation just presented, the consultant had inadvertently placed a stumbling block of perception in the way of the finance and sales managers. The stumbling block was the simpler and positive story told in Figure 6.3: That of the customer service team's increasing volume of contacts handled *and* the increasing usage of the new system.

Visually, the upward trending lines and growing size of the stacked area chart set an overall positive story in the context of the customer service team's adoption of the new system. That positive story was then associated with that style of chart, regardless of the story told by the actual data in a different context. When the finance and sales managers encountered a very similar chart with a far different story in Figure 6.4 their apparent reliance on the availability of previous positive story telling was their initial perception of the data. Unfortunately, the negative story contained in the adoption percentages displayed of Figure 6.4 were now not perceptually weighted as heavily as the overall visual image was in the minds of these managers.

In this situation, it would be wise to follow the inverse of the Law of Continuity (Chapter 2) in order to display the disparity in the relationships of the data being considered. Rather than placing the percentage of adoption of the new system along the same trend line as the volume of contacts or volume of deals put through the new system, the percentages should be shown on a second axis, or even better, on a second chart. Another confounding problem hindering the Availability Bias of the managers was the difference in counting methodologies between the two charts. Figure 6.3 displays counts on the y-axis of the total contacts by customers to the customer service center per month. In this chart such a count is easy to understand and provides a static reference from one month to the next; every month begins at zero contacts and increases as customers contact Acme Medical throughout the month. However, in Figure 6.4 the count on the y-axis is of outstanding deals per month. In this chart the count of outstanding deals is not static per month—it could be greater or fewer deals rolling over from one month to the next—and additional new deals are likely being added to the system as each month of the year progresses. The count of deals in Figure 6.4 has both process and business decisions embedded in the explanation of why the count is what it is each month.

6.4 Informed Redesign

After the consultant explained these factors to the sales and finance managers, the managers suggested a more granular set of charts be developed to identify which sales representatives were most active in the system, who was having the most success using the new system, and whether there were differences in the type of deals being put through the system for each group. The consultant determined that rather than provide confusing, time-variant activity on top of this level of detail, a snapshot of current state deals would be best for explaining the variances between the sales and finance teams.

Figure 6.5, top and bottom panels, highlights the discrepancy in the number of deals per sales rep (with the three finance analysts shown as sales representatives) based on the status of all outstanding deals in upper panel of Figure 6.5, and all cumulative deals closed in the lower panel. From this information it becomes more apparent that the finance team is creating, modifying and completing more deals than the average sales representative. The next visualization that the consultant prepared relied on system timestamp information to provide a snapshot of the length of time that outstanding deals had been in an open status on the system.

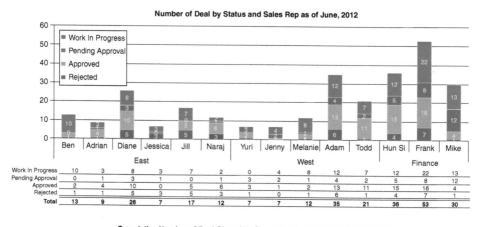

Number of Deal by Status and Sales Rep as of June, 2012

	Ben	Adrian	Diane	Jessica	Jill	Naraj	Yuri	Jenny	Melanie	Adam	Todd	Hun Si	Frank	Mike
	East						West					Finance		
Work In Progress	10	3	8	3	7	2	0	4	8	12	7	12	22	13
Pending Approval	0	1	3	1	0	1	3	2	1	4	2	5	8	12
Approved	2	4	10	0	5	6	3	1	2	13	11	15	16	4
Rejected	1	1	5	3	5	3	1	0	1	6	1	4	7	1
Total	13	9	26	7	17	12	7	7	12	35	21	36	53	30

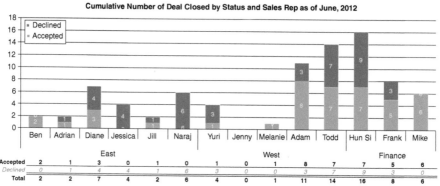

Cumulative Number of Deal Closed by Status and Sales Rep as of June, 2012

	Ben	Adrian	Diane	Jessica	Jill	Naraj	Yuri	Jenny	Melanie	Adam	Todd	Hun Si	Frank	Mike
	East						West					Finance		
Accepted	2	1	3	0	1	0	1	0	1	8	7	7	5	6
Declined	0	1	4	4	1	6	3	0	0	3	7	9	3	0
Total	2	2	7	4	2	6	4	0	1	11	14	16	8	6

FIGURE 6.5 Number of Deals and Cumulative Number Closed by Status and Sales Rep

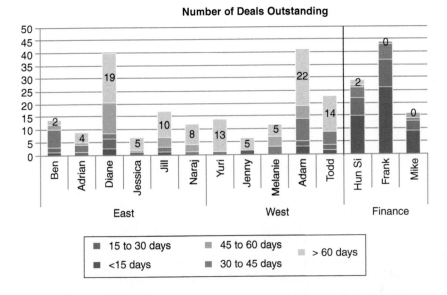

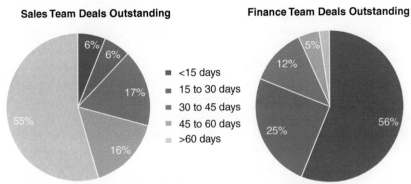

FIGURE 6.6 Deals Outstanding by Number of Days Outstanding

Here the discrepancy between the sales team and the finance team becomes even more apparent. The length of time that it was taking the sales representatives to move a deal through the system is much greater.

Armed with these new depictions of the data, the consultant presented these visualizations to the sales and finance managers. Both managers now understood why both of their teams had been complaining about the system. The sales representatives thought using the new tool took far too long to get a deal to the stage where it could be presented to the customer for a final decision. The finance team felt that the sales representatives were leaning too heavily on the finance team's expertise to prepare complex deals that could have been handled directly by the sales representatives using the system.

Another outcome of these charts were that the managers began sharing these visualizations with their team members each month. Within three months, two of the least productive sales representatives had resigned, and both teams had improved deal turnaround time by an average of 15 days (an improvement of 20 percent). Further questions remained which the consultant was tasked with answering, but the initial learning achieved by all parties had contributed to making Acme Medical a growing success in the new marketplace of long-term care medical rehabilitation equipment sales and service.

6.5   Lessons for Future Development

This hypothetical story of data visualization in a sales organization illustrates how human perception can not only present stumbling blocks, but also focal points for leveraging design principles. In each example, there was a happy ending since no one decision resulted in catastrophic mistakes being made. Deliberative decision-making is most effective under business conditions involving complex problems and ongoing efforts to capture value for an organization. Careful data visualization design is preferred to non-codified heuristic decision-making; however, heuristic decision-making approaches can still be more effective under time-sensitive, emotionally charged or potentially dangerous conditions even if the outcomes are less than perfect.

The goal in a business context is to strike an appropriate balance between non-codified heuristic approaches and a structured/objective system of data visualizations. Furthermore, presenting systems of visuals of key performance indicators can be powerful motivators for an entire organization to align strategy with front-line employee actions (as noted by Kaplan and Norton 1996) (see Figure 6.6). How does one do this? By ongoing study and curiosity of how data might be visualized in an evolving system of visuals, and how the presentation of that data is interpreted and used for decision-making. Relying on what has worked in the past or in only visualizing data to support heuristic decision-making assumptions tends to result in sub-optimal decision-making. The consultant in this story would do well to look for new opportunities to improve managerial decision-making and employee behaviors with additional data combinations and visualizations.

References

Bendoly, E., M. Cotteleer. 2008. Understanding behavioral sources of process variation following enterprise system deployment. *Journal of Operations Management* 26(1), 23–44.

Cotteleer, M., E. Bendoly. 2006. Order lead-time improvement following enterprise-IT implementation: an empirical study. *MIS Quarterly* 30(3), 643–660.

Friedman, W.A. 1998. John H. Patterson and the sales strategy of the National Cash Register Company, 1884 to 1922. *Business History Review* 72(4), 552.

Kaplan, R.S. and Norton, D.P. 1996. *The Balanced Scorecard: Translating Strategy into Action.* Boston, MA: Harvard Business School Press, p. 29.

7
FRAMING WICKED PROBLEMS USING CO-DESIGN AND A HYBRID DESIGN TOOLSET

Erika Braun

The term "wicked problem," first introduced by Horst Rittel and Melvin Webber, refers to problems that are difficult or impossible to solve because of incomplete and often contradictory information, and changing requirements that are difficult to recognize and organize. There is no way of determining a "right" solution because "every wicked problem can be considered to be a symptom of another problem" (Rittel and Webber 1973; Kolko 2012). Consequently, these problems are often multi-faceted and wrapped in ambiguous causal webs that rely on iterative problem solving approaches.

One such example is captured by the interrelated tasks of (a) assessing the needs of transitioning adults on the autism spectrum and (b) identifying design opportunities for the Center for Autism Services and Transition (CAST) at The Ohio State University Wexner Medical Center (OSUWMC) focusing on a patient-centered healthcare experience. This challenge involves multiple stakeholders with differing goals and needs, incomplete or contradictory information, and no idealized solution or end-state. Transitional care and support for adults with autism and their families is part of a macro-web of interconnected issues that reach far beyond physical healthcare.

The dominant approach leveraged here was that of Participatory Action Research (PAR), an iterative co-design process focused on shared learning, shared knowledge, and collaborative analysis among the stakeholders who help to shape the outcome (Howard and Somerville 2014). Unlike Participatory Design approaches (Sanders et al. 2010), PAR is an action-oriented, learning-centered, co-design approach aimed at producing "knowledge and action directly useful to people, and also to empower people through the process of constructing and using their own knowledge" (Shortall 2003). It is an approach used in design to conduct research "by, for and with the people who will benefit from it, leading to making practical improvements or transformations" to their current situation.

Design has the potential to shape the way people behave, how they gather information and acquire knowledge, how they communicate across barriers and how they interact with one another. Using a PAR process together with data visualizations and various methods/tools of Design Thinking, this case study centered on bringing stakeholders together, not to passively share their thoughts, needs, and ideas, but to become immersed in the wicked problem, actively contribute unique perspectives, collectively reframe the scope, and co-design new resolutions aimed at creating true value at the clinic and optimizing care for transitioning adults and their families. The aim was not to determine a single design solution for the autism clinic, but instead to use abductive reasoning (Dorst 2011) and collective sensemaking to look at the problem in a new way and help the integral stakeholders be a part of the solution by bringing them into co-design roles and providing tools and spaces through which new knowledge, insights, and understanding could be engendered collaboratively.

This idea aligns with Weick's (1988) discussions of enacted sensemaking, and in particular Bendoly's (2016) extension of that discussion with regards to data-visual support tools. In exploring the potential of technology in PAR and the expanding role of designers as form givers and visual translators not only to design outcomes, but also in framing a problem and shaping the "seeing" and "making" tools for collaborative action, a blended interaction prototype (digital tool) was developed for collective sensemaking in parallel with the autism case study (Victor 2015). Blended interaction incorporates the use of touch devices in shared spaces. Through a combination of embodied interactions, social interactions, and the elements of "play" on a shared digital device, blended interaction tools can promote a shared experience of engagement, understanding, and collective expression (Jetter et al. 2012). Technology can equip designers and co-designers with new ways of seeing, interacting, and organizing data in order to collectively determine the scope of the problem and identify more meaningful frames through which innovative resolutions can emerge. The role of technology in this case study was to translate qualitative research data that had been extrapolated from multiple resources and perspectives and present it on a malleable touch platform through which the diverse team of designers and co-designers could provide context, draw connections between priority needs and opportunities, and together construct a new map of understanding and a visual representation of the frame of the wicked problem through which true value could be created. The case study asserts the value of the "human contribution" in sensemaking.

7.1 Appreciating the Audience and Context

People make sense by extrapolating information from the world around them in an attempt to gain understanding. In this case study, the data we extrapolated came from secondary research, as well as from the personal and second-hand experiences of a diverse group of stakeholders connected to the wicked problem: adults on the autism spectrum, parents, and healthcare providers/administrators, who shared their thoughts, needs, and ideas in interviews, surveys, and focus group sessions in Phase 1. Individually, the goals across all stakeholder groups for this project (reported on an initial questionnaire) centered on gaining skills and knowledge to feel more empowered to help others on the spectrum and their families, to learn from other stakeholders and gain new understanding, being an active participant, and helping to make a difference for families and people with autism, and to be heard—having an opportunity to share their challenges and unique perspectives with other stakeholders. Collectively, they hoped that we (the collective team) would become more informed, that there would be open dialogue between the stakeholders so ideas and knowledge could be shared, and that we could develop meaningful ideas and actionable next steps.

Prior to participation, there had been limited communication between the stakeholder groups. Those on the autism spectrum had not had an opportunity to voice their needs or ideas since they were spoken for on behalf of parents and healthcare providers. Every stakeholder had their own vision for the clinic and views of the problems facing adults on the spectrum and their families, but limited understanding of the needs of other stakeholders connected to the wicked problem or how to tackle it. Some of the questions that needed to be addressed concerned the gaps and missed opportunities in the current clinic and local Autism Spectrum Disorder (ASD) network, determining how to create true value in the new clinic and make it sustainable, how to improve the network for a more patient-centered model, and how to prioritize diverging goals and ideas among the stakeholders.

Data visualizations are often represented in a system of interactive (non-static) idioms (or graphic depictions) designed to convey a story (Bendoly 2016). However, in the case of a multi-faceted wicked problem, the conveyance of a single story may not provide stakeholders with enough information. Often what appears to be left out of data visualizations is the context behind the visual artifact. Dr. Elliot Bendoly (2016) asserts that data visualizations should be a continuous process of understanding, instead of being viewed simply as an outcome. Technology and visualizations were integrated into this case study to support the sensemaking abilities of the designers and co-designers in giving context to the problem and to build shared understanding. The digital tool prototype was intended to help the co-designers build context into the data that had been collected and together build a frame of reference and understanding regarding the wicked problem and the value we should be creating for this wicked problem through design.

Furthermore, the value of a visualization is measured by its ability to convey meaning. When people have the same frame of reference, translation and meaning are quickly grasped. The designer and the stakeholders in this case study came from different backgrounds and experiences. In order to present the various perspectives and priority concerns, needs, and goals of each stakeholder group that were collected in Phase 1, an interactive visualization prototype was designed to allow the stakeholders to see inside the wicked problem and across possibilities by interacting with data points (needs/goals), and together draw connections/ relationships between the priority issues/opportunities on a shared multi-touch device.

Because CAST and the related problems associated with transitional care and support for adults with autism and their families are wicked, there was no idealized end-state or right or wrong way of reaching a final outcome or solution. Instead there was an opportunity to use visualization tools and design methods to help stakeholders establish a common language and collectively learn, share, and explore through one another and the tools ways to improve the situation. The purpose of the digital visualization prototype for PAR was to be able to present collected research data in a flexible manner and explore how a collective group could use the tool to communicate perspectives and visually see and record evolving thought processes, while jointly building connections among prioritized data and engaging with each other through shared interactions. The digital prototype was intended to provide visual feedback on shared thoughts and data patterns/relationships, and also be able to communicate that process to stakeholders after the session, or to newcomers who were not able to be present by capturing manipulations on the screen and documenting the evolution of thought through video.

Most data analytics tools read big data and provide the "end of the story" through a visual diagram or chart. What is missing in these tools (and the final outcomes) is context—"why" are the patterns the way they are? Bringing all of the stakeholders together to explain and show which need/goal they prioritized and how it may or may not have been connected to another stakeholder group's priority, gave context and meaning to the visualization (or "visual narrative") that was created collectively. An interactive data tool can help designers and co-designers visualize, structure, and reframe systems-based problems collectively, diagram connections between needs and assumptions, bring opposing views together, and most importantly to act as a catalyzer of action during the sensemaking process.

7.2   Design Principles Applied

The role of the designer in this case study encompassed not only facilitation of Design Thinking methods and tools through co-design, but also that of curator, bricoleur (Wright 2005), and problem architect—helping to give form to the wicked problem. In those roles, the designer created the seeing/maker spaces and tools through which the co-designers could express thoughts and ideas, gain shared understanding, and experience new forms of problem solving and critical making (Ratto 2011). Qualitative data assembled and interpreted from Phase 1 was then translated into visualizations and the interactive digital tool prototype. Through these mediums the data was turned into useful, usable, and desirable information for the collective sessions.

The digital visualization prototype designed for the case study blended interaction on a multi-touch table, so that each data point could be manipulated and rearranged on the table freely by the stakeholders. Beyond creating beautiful, colorful graphics and playful interfaces, the prototype was used to identify patterns and outliers in the wicked problem, stimulate new ways of thinking, serve as a working model from which to iterate and evolve the frame of the problem. It was also intended to transparently communicate thoughts and decisions throughout the process of sensemaking (Chapter 3). Phase 1 data (needs and goals) were presented in a non-linear way on round nodes, all similar in size, positioned in a circle on the multi-touch screen. The data was presented in this way to prevent initial assumptions or biases, and instead to immerse co-designers in the design synthesis process (the process designers often use to make sense of research before ideation). Additionally, the interactive tool was designed to encourage active participation and stimulate a sense of investigation, a desire to collectively seek out and build context and new relationships and hierarchies among malleable data points in order to determine what issues were most relevant for tackling the wicked problem in the most meaningful way.

During Phase 1, visualizations were incorporated into the interviews to provoke further/deeper discussions. The visualizations served as provotypes, or provocative prototypes, (Boer and Donovan 2012) from which the stakeholders could iteratively define present needs and explore new possibilities. In each interview, patient journey maps and visual concepts for the clinic were iterated. Focus group sessions applied a blend of exploratory and generative design research methods like problem probing, visual mapping/diagramming, identifying needs and goals, and sharing scenarios to help the stakeholders express their needs and goals around the clinic and within the realm of transitions and adult care/support.

The interviews, prototypes, and focus groups were designed to gain a better understanding of the autism network/topic, to help each stakeholder group organize their thoughts and create a compelling case to the others, and to provide data that would be integrated into the interactive data visualization prototype for collective sensemaking. The qualitative information shared and the visualizations created in Phase 1 became the content of stakeholder presentations that were shared at the beginning of Workshop 1. The presentations, co-designed with members of each stakeholder group, were designed to communicate unique perspectives through personal narratives, visual illustrations, and comparative visual maps.

The priorities and perspectives shared by each stakeholder group during Phase 1 were the result of Availability Bias. They also encompassed the perceptions parents and healthcare providers/administrators initially had of the needs of adults with autism. However, these perceptions were quickly widened through the inclusion of adults on the spectrum in this project who had an opportunity to self-advocate and share their perspectives and ideas, along with the other stakeholder groups. Presentations, given by representatives from each stakeholder group at the beginning of Phase 2 prior to collective sensemaking and visual mapping, were integrated into the PAR framework in an effort to democratize the collaborative session by giving each group an equal voice. Simultaneously, the presentations were designed to expand and broaden the scope of the stakeholders, in an effort to derive more shared understanding during the sensemaking session that followed. Shared understanding generated through the presentations helped to reduce individual biases and appeared to make the sensemaking session that followed more collaborative, because the collective was now looking through a much broader lens. However, Causal Bias was observed in the weight given to the thoughts expressed by the ASD participants because their needs and ideas were new and had not yet been heard, only assumed. Their input, along with the parents, had an impact on how issues were prioritized and how the participants chose to make sense of the wicked problem in the sensemaking session.

All of the data collected in Phase 1 was qualitative and messy. In addition to being incorporated into the content of the presentations, the data was grouped into twenty-four needs and twenty-four goals, which were organized into eight categories in an Excel spreadsheet. Using a program named Unity (typically used for 3D animation and game development), each need/goal was translated from a line of data in Excel to a round node. The initial forty-eight needs/goals served as constraints, to promote convergence and to draw stakeholders together to frame meaning, instead of diverge and generate ideas. The goal was not for the designer to create a visual summary from the needs/goals that had been collected in Phase 1, but instead to design a tool through which the collective could express their thoughts, reprioritize the issues that were relevant, and bring together multiple data points to form a new whole, a new visual map (narrative) of the problem scope collectively.

Correct or incorrect, the construction of a new map of understanding during the sensemaking session was built by the participants who were present and the perspectives that had been shared. By the end of the sensemaking session it was evident that the co-designers felt there was more to lose in not identifying and tackling long-term, disruptive innovation opportunities associated with the wellbeing of adults with autism and their families in multiple aspects of their lives, than there was to gain by focusing our efforts on redesigning the clinic specifically. Through shared understanding and sensemaking, the co-designers had discovered larger root problems beyond the clinic and were therefore more motivated to tackle issues that could have a disruptive impact or long-term effect on ASD and the transitions problem, rather than address low-risk, near-term issues in the clinic. From this new frame of reference we repositioned the scope of the third phase of the project to building prototypes and visualizing ideal futures that centered on maximizing the potential of adults with autism and their parents, as well as promoting self-advocacy and peace of mind.

Workshop 2 was designed to bridge sensemaking and action-taking through early prototyping and concept development. Four key themes emerged from the sensemaking session and were explored further in Workshop 2: accessibility and continuous care and support, long-term planning, improving navigation, and socialization interaction. Within each of these four themes were a list of long-term ideas and near-term ideas that had been expressed by co-designers throughout Phases 1 and 2. Through persona development, prospective scenario mapping, and prototyping in Workshop 2 (Phase 3), the co-designers imagined better futures for adults on the spectrum and ideated around disruptive resolutions that would help to support the needs and nurture the potential of adults with ASD and their families.

7.3 Examination of Use

An early prototype of the digital data visualization tool was tested in Workshop 1. Various stakeholders (including those with ASD) curiously approached the multi-touch table, interested in playing with it and interacting with the data. The table was connected to a projector that conveyed the interactions onto a large whiteboard wall. Representatives from each stakeholder group used the digital prototype to denote their top ten need/goal nodes from the forty-eight topics. The touch interface of the screen afforded the ability for co-designers to select and drag nodes out from the original circle and regroup them. Additionally, stakeholder icons could be added to the nodes to increase their size and convey priority (while at the same time depicting which stakeholder(s) had selected the node as a priority). Connector dots were attached to each node, allowing lines to be drawn between them. The function of drawing lines was intended to prompt the collective team to define the relationship between the nodes and any feedback loops in the wicked problem (e.g. did one need or goal impact or inform another need/goal in the system?), not just prioritize issues that needed to be addressed. The line function served as a way for the group to identify root problems and also determine gaps (needs/goals that were unconnected that should be linked). Flexible positioning and clustering of the nodes, along with prioritization and connector lines, allowed co-designers to begin constructing a new map (or visual narrative) together to provide more context to the wicked problem and how their expressed needs and goals were connected. While constructing the map, screen images were taken and stored in a file every fifteen seconds to capture the progression of the decisions that were being made. The intent was to compile these images into a video to share with the stakeholders after the session.

Participants who were not physically interacting with the touch table referred to the projected interactions and discussed the priorities that were being made visible. The group got as far as prioritizing the topics and drawing connections when the digital tool malfunctioned. It was not until later testing, after the workshop session, that a technical glitch was identified in the function of deleting the connector lines.

Forty-eight circular sticky notes (matching the colors and shapes in the digital tool) were used on the whiteboard wall to continue the visual sensemaking (mapping) process. The needs/goals that had been prioritized by the stakeholder groups were written on larger, circular sticky notes. Participants who had gathered around the touch table stepped back and the act of clustering and drawing connections between the note topics was handed back over to the design facilitators. The participants provided direction as the prioritized notes were regrouped into hierarchies and common themes. After the prioritized needs/goals were clustered, the group discussed how the node topics within the clusters and across clusters were connected. Through reclustering, prioritization, and connecting, the design facilitators and co-designers developed a new visual narrative and a new frame for the wicked problem.

7.4 Informed Redesign

The presentations, along with the digital and non-digital mapping tools, brought about a broader understanding through storytelling, mutual sharing, and collective sensemaking. Insights gained through the process of sticky note mapping on the whiteboard wall and discoveries made while fixing the glitch in the digital tool informed the design of new features and led to a solution that would allow data to be brought into the tool more readily. Problems tackled through trial and error play-testing (after the workshop) became opportunities to expand capabilities of the prototype and make it more robust. One of the new features, inspired by the actions of the participants during the session, was the addition of customizable idea nodes. On multiple occasions ideas had been expressed simultaneously with needs. The revised tool currently allows new ideas to be captured with and connected to reorganized and reprioritized needs and goals. Additionally, a "suggested" cluster feature was added based on the proximity placement of one node to another. Now, when nodes are dragged within a certain range to one another, a dotted circle materializes around the nodes to point out potential themes, hierarchies, and relationships. Users are then given the choice to create a new custom cluster. Directional arrows and animated line segments were added to visually show cause and effect hierarchy as well as the type of correlation between the nodes. The organization of node clusters, hierarchy, and directional arrows creates more linear relationships, aimed at giving constructed narratives more clarity.

The revised digital tool was used to reenact the actions and decisions that had taken place using the sticky notes. The screen captures were then compiled into a video and sent out to the stakeholders along with photographs of the final sticky note map to show our progression of thought. Screen captures of the revised digital tool are pictured below. The blue dots represent needs, the green dots are goals, the red dot represents idea nodes (customizable by participants), and the purple dots are connector dots from which connector lines can be drawn.

Red "idea" nodes are housed on the right side of the screen in Figure 7.1. The gray icons pictured on the left side of the screen represent each stakeholder group. As stakeholder icons are added, the nodes grow in size, helping to visualize prioritization among the topic nodes (Figure 7.2).

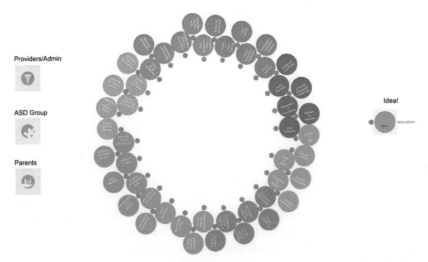

FIGURE 7.1 The Initial Circle of Nodes (needs/goals by varying stakeholders from Phase 1)

FIGURE 7.2 Using the Stakeholder Icons to Visually Indicate Prioritization

Once nodes have been prioritized they can be removed from the original circle. Familiar scale, rotate, and drag touch gestures are connected to the wheel of original nodes. These features allow the wheel to be read from all sides, and reduced in size and moved out of the way to create a more blank canvas on which to design a new visual narrative (see lower right corner Figure 7.2).

A potential trap with this digital prototype is that once nodes are removed and prioritized (scaled up) with stakeholder icons, it is easy to overlook the needs/goals that were not selected. Bias emerges once scale is introduced and nodes are selected. While the other nodes were initially expressed and important in Phase 1, these nodes were pushed aside to make room for the new visual representation that was being created, based on priorities and patterns (sensemaking) being done by those that were present. This may pose a problem, especially to newcomers who may value some of the needs/goals that were not selected. Especially in a wicked problem, where iterative understanding and ideation are important, a digital tool for sensemaking should support continuous input from multiple perspectives over time. Further development needs to be conducted with the digital prototype to explore ways to incorporate a time-lapse feature (beyond just a playback feature to retrace decisions) that would allow newcomers to rewind decisions that were made at different points in time and make adjustments/additions to those decisions, instead of working from where the map was last completed.

7.5   Lessons for Future Development

Collaborating stakeholders and designers in the future may benefit from the use of an interactive digital tool, similar to the one developed with this case study, to organize and communicate complex data, translate multi-faceted problems into a systems narrative, and to help them to visualize their progressive thought processes. Visually seeing priorities, themes, feedback loops and disconnects between unmet needs/goals and addressing them collectively on a shared work surface may help to facilitate understanding and shared engagement to act on a complex issue.

In the brief time spent using the early version of the visualization tool on the multi-touch surface, the stakeholders appeared more curious about interacting with the data and the tool than they were using sticky notes. The interactive surface offered a game-like experience that made the data, that otherwise could have seemed overwhelming and messy, perhaps more appealing. Additionally, the digital prototype offered a new type of experience that engaged participants in a new way of interacting with each other and the information surrounding the wicked problem. Data visualized in an interactive way (whether it is in a digital tool or on a wall) allows the user to see patterns, simulate multiple frames, and make sense of data they may otherwise have seemed intimidating.

The early prototype of the digital tool was able to collect, manipulate, share, and store data, as well as record the interactions of the stakeholders, but the technology was unreliable. The benefit of sticky notes and the paper data-mapping processes is that they are more dependable, however the data cannot be easily manipulated, stored, or recorded for future use. The value of a digital tool for mapping is traceability, allowing real-time decisions to easily be shared with others in follow-up sessions or discussions, and impermanence, the ability to simulate multiple situations. The digital visualization tool afforded the co-designers the ability to readily show variations and changes in the perception of the data as decisions were being made. With paper-based tools it can be harder to quickly highlight priorities with similarly sized sticky notes, or to suggest new ways of reorganizing the data using static materials. In addition to altering the scale of prioritized nodes, Figure 7.3 demonstrates how new themes can be generated based on the proximity of where the nodes are placed (intentionally or unintentionally) by the collaborators on the screen.

The participants have the ultimate influence over the decision to make the suggested cluster a definitive new group by selecting the checkmark. Custom names can be given to each group and connection lines can be drawn to show relationships between nodes inside and outside of the groups, as shown in Figures 7.4 and 7.5. The red idea nodes (pictured on the right of the screen in Figure 7.3) can be added/customized any time during the process of analysis and synthesis. These features balance structure (initial data points) and the flexibility to add new content during sensemaking.

The use of paper tools to visualize and make sense of data is relegated to co-located, real-time experiences. Along with being more interactive, the digital tool affords users the ability to record, rewind, or fast-forward actions, allowing the experience to occur across time and space. Prior to the final phase of the project, a video of what we had done collectively with the sticky notes on the whiteboard wall was recreated using the revised digital tool prototype and sent to each participant. Participants were able to view a video of the entire mapping/connecting process, which helped to explain how new themes and connections were formed and what decisions were being reframed around the wicked problem.

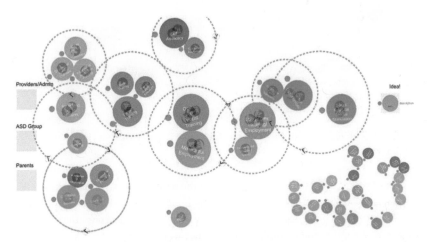

FIGURE 7.3 Suggested Clusters (gray) Formed When Nodes are Placed Near to One Another

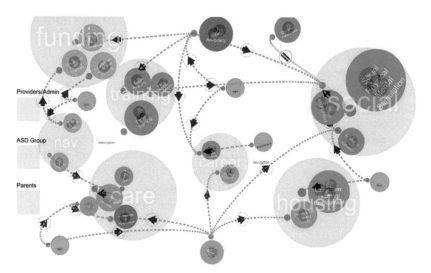

FIGURE 7.4 The Addition of New "Red" Ideas and Connector Dots, Allowing Linkage—I

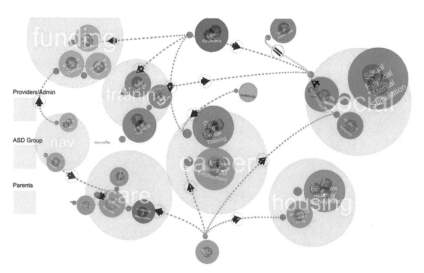

FIGURE 7.5 The Addition of New "Red" Ideas and Connector Dots, Allowing Linkage—II

A post-project questionnaire was given to the participants after Workshop 2 (the final phase involving the prototyping of new concepts) to gauge how much they had learned, what goals had been achieved, and whether they saw merit in using visualizations and Design Thinking approaches to tackle future wicked problems. Results indicated that the participants valued the Design Thinking process we used and gained new understanding of the needs related to adults on the spectrum and their families, as well as the challenges faced by providers in the healthcare system. Most felt more empowered to make changes to the current situation, were more confident and interested in collaboration, and maintained that there is value in gaining shared understanding, prototyping, and using visualizations to better understand complex problems. While human–computer interaction and technology can offer certain advantages to extend sensemaking across time and space and promote learning through collective making, it is important to note that there is also value in designing PAR tools that afford hands-on making and face-to-face (human to human) interaction for shared learning and understanding.

A hybrid toolset can be invaluable to a shared learning experience. Participants found value in presenting face-to-face (having an opportunity to share and listen to different perspectives) to establish empathy first, prior to mapping collaboratively (on a shared surface) and collectively reframing the problem. They also found value and making personas and prototypes together in Phase 3. Through this project the participants expressed appreciation for their perspectives and ideas that were taken into consideration and for the exposure to new problem solving approaches through the methods and tools that were used, which helped them to gain new awareness. While playing an active role in co-design, the stakeholders made steps towards implementing more practical solutions, cross-fertilizing new knowledge, and connecting with each other.

The outcomes of this project were both tangible (relating to new resolutions and design artifacts) and intangible (relating to feelings and knowledge), and addressed both near and long-term goals. Throughout the PAR process the expectation was that we would generate tangible concepts that were connected to discovered unmet needs and opportunities. The tangible outcomes that were brought up and/or prototyped ranged from products to environments, communication, and service concepts. They included resources to improve patient/doctor relationships, tools to connect/integrate provider networks, and train providers (inside and outside the realm of special needs).

An online resource and self-advocacy platform was prototyped to help parents and people on the spectrum connect with each other and resources (like housing and jobs) specifically tailored to their needs. Additionally, visual navigation on this site, along with tools in the clinic, were proposed to help guide patients and their families through not only the healthcare facility, but also to guide them along their child's life journey (knowing what to anticipate and expect to create peace of mind—near and long term). Adults on the spectrum shared resolutions to improve the "waiting" experience at the clinic and make it less stressful, as well as ideas to create "safe" social gaming environments for neurotypicals and people with ASD to connect around shared interests. Lastly, improved healthcare tools and services were proposed to improve navigation and make the communication channels more fluid in transitional care between pediatric and adult ASD medical care providers, as well as outside specialists.

The intangible outcomes that emerged over the course of the PAR process were unexpected. A sense of belonging, empathy and shared understanding, and empowerment were perceived and expressed by the stakeholders throughout the sessions. For a parent, "engagement, awareness, encouragement, and a sense of community" came out of the sessions. "There was a realization that there is a broader community than we thought and that we can work together to solve this complex problem." The participants with ASD believed that the resolutions designed for them should not be designed without their inclusion and input. Bringing the participants with ASD into PAR gave them an opportunity to share their expertise and become vital members of the process. The visualization tools and design methods gave the stakeholders a platform through which to voice thoughts and express feelings, as well as create new possibilities, while also encouraging the diverse team to participate in new ways of problem solving and experiencing perspectives beyond their individual frames of reference.

"New ways of thinking arose. New connections were made. These connections can lead to future collaborations," said a parent. The beauty with collecting data in a flexible digital space is that it can be referred to later. The interactions and connections made in the sensemaking session can be recreated in future sessions and built upon with new teams. Information on sticky notes tends to get placed in a corner and never referred to again. Data presented to the collective through interactive nodes afforded them an opportunity to freely position and regroup the data in new and different ways, to help them see the problem from multiple viewpoints, and review their actions/decisions after the session. Instead of presenting the Excel data in a matrix or as a static visual summary that only provided one point of view, the collective group was able to simulate different relationships and patterns and determine a new frame for the problem situation through shared engagement on a blended interaction tool. Both near and far-term concepts that emerged from this project will require additional "experts" and resources. Data captured and stored interactively in a digital tool will extend the reach of the sensemaking that has taken place so far. The connections and actions that need to be achieved at different levels of opportunities will become clearer as new co-design teams are assembled around the resolutions to carry them into the next stage of design and development.

References

Bendoly, E. (2016). Fit, bias and enacted sensemaking in data visualization: frameworks for continuous in operations and supply chain management analytics. *Journal of Business Logistics* 37(1): 6–17.

Boer, L., and Donovan, J. (2012). Provotypes for participatory innovation. In *Proceedings of the Designing Interactive Systems Conference.* ACM, June, 388–397.

Dorst, K. 2011. The core of "design thinking" and its application. *Design Studies* 32(6): 521–532.

Howard, Z., and Somerville, M.M. (2014). A comparative study of two design charrettes: implications for codesign and participatory action research. *CoDesign* 10(1): 46–62.

Jetter, H., Geyer, F., Schwarz, T., and Reiterer, H. (2012). Blended interaction – toward a framework for the design of interactive spaces. In *Workshop DCIS*, vol. 12.

Kolko, J. (2012). *Wicked problems: Problems worth solving: A handbook and call to action.* Austin, TX: Austin Center for Design.

Ratto, M. (2011). Critical making: conceptual and material studies in technology and social life. *The Information Society* 27(4): 252–260.

Rittel, H.W.J., and Webber, M.M. (1973). Dilemmas in a general theory of planning. *Policy Sciences* 4(2): 155–169.

Sanders, E.B-N., Brandt, E., and Binder, T. (2010). A framework for organizing the tools and techniques of participatory design. In *Proceedings of the 11th Biennial Participatory Design Conference.* ACM, 195–198.

Shortall, S. (2003). *Participatory action research. The AZ of social research*, New York, NY: Sage, 225–227.

Victor, B. (2015). Seeing Spaces. Beast of Burden. http://worrydream.com/, accessed October 30, 2015.

Weick, K. (1988). Enacted sensemaking in crisis situations. *Journal of Management Studies* 25(4): 305–317.

Wright, A. (2005). The role of scenarios as prospective sensemaking devices. *Management Decision* 43(1): 86–101.

8
VISUAL SUPPORT FOR COMPLEX REPAIR OPERATIONS IN A GLOBAL AEROSPACE COMPANY

Sian Joel-Edgar, Lei Shi, Lia Emanuel, Simon Jones, Leon Watts, Linda Newnes, Stephen Payne, Ben Hicks and Stephen Culley

Project managers are often faced with operational processes that are complex and difficult to monitor (Bititci et al. 2012). Project teams can be geographically distributed, have contextual differences between projects and such teams may face issues that are temporal in nature (Bendoly 2014; Shi et al. 2014b). Monitoring the progression of active projects, and specifically how projects evolve over their workflow, can be of vital importance. Further, understanding whether a project is following the best possible projected pathway, and being able to identify possible delays in the project early on, empowers operations teams to take actions and evaluate impacts. Such understanding is becoming increasingly relevant where Service Level Agreements (SLAs) are in place. In SLA settings in particular, shifts in performance can alert a project manager to a potential threat to operational plans. Conversely, a lack of such awareness can result in embedded errors and project cost and/or time overruns (Hicks 2013). Assessing project performance can be challenging, as a number of factors affect the evaluation of the performance indicators and overall output of the project (Carey et al. 2013; Xie et al. 2011).

8.1 Appreciating the Audience and Context

Contextual issues, such as understanding the inner associations among project components, can be fundamentally problematic. Typically, large projects will contain many teams, sub-systems and inter-connected processes within an organization. Once a project becomes large and/or highly distributed, it is difficult for internal team members to fully appreciate the detail of the project, make sense of how various components are inter-linked, and understand the effect of these connections on the overall project.

Along with the complexity of these contexts, difficulties often arise in the fragmented or distributed nature of project information and data. This often emerges when data is drawn from multiple persons, departments and timeframes. Such fragmentation can result in signals that are inconsistent or inaccurate (as per the discussion in Chapter 1). Simultaneously, project data can also be imposing in that often a vast amount of data can be stored over a project and organization's lifespan; and not always data of the type or in the form needed by the project managers. The digital footprint of a project can be broad, inter-connected, complex and rich, with enormous potential value. Legacy data from previous systems and historical projects can also be difficult to manage, assess and incorporate into on-going analyses. However, making sense of all data sources will be time-consuming and the conclusions of such efforts uncertain. Frequently these efforts are carried out without the necessary analytical expertise and tool support to make use of it. This results in data selection processes that bring with them further challenge (as per the discussion in Chapter 2).

To be sure, it is important to preserve and re-use expert knowledge, where it exists. Any analysis of project data and performance evaluation requires some degree of judgment, given the operational context in which it is to be exercised. It is highly likely that the validity of such judgments is more secure if the decision maker is an experienced participant in the domain of the project to which the data pertains. Consequently, expert knowledge and assessment is crucially important in the interpretation of performance indicators.

The challenges of evaluation indictors for complex information such as that described above are inextricably linked to factors affecting data visualization in project management. These challenges are relevant to all industries. Overcoming these challenges requires a deliberate level of care and scrutiny.

8.2 Design Principles Applied

KPIs have been shown to be an effective way to monitor and improve management performance and execution in collaborative projects (Parmenter 2010). Broadly KPIs follow the "Iron Triangle" model of cost, time and quality; these three factors have been used to assess project performance by a number of management approaches (Atkinson 1999). However the Iron Triangle model struggles to encompass large projects with complex structures. The application of identical performance indicators across different teams, organizational structures and operational performance is often doomed to fail. Performance indicators can have radically different meanings as they reflect different project objectives, requirements, resources, conditions and stakeholder perspectives (Bryde 2005; Lauras et al. 2010). Thus the presence of such data can represent additional problems of interpretation for project managers: just what do they really indicate and how important might that be, given the value and status of the project for which they are responsible? As a result, it is clear that additional or alternative information is needed to address the operational complexity of project performance, supporting the on-the-ground expertise of team members.

Recent research has sought to identify additional categories of information that may be treated as indicators of other project-critical dimensions, including budget, schedule adherence, satisfaction, technical specifications, and health and safety (Chan and Chan 2004; Pheng and Chuan 2006; Toor and Ogunlana 2010). Meanwhile, the high-level interpretation of such indicators has been further extended to a more detailed level, including project efficiency, impact on the customer, direct business success/organizational success and resilience, among other measures (Lauras et al. 2010). In contrast to traditional indicators these provide details about activities/processes in real time, and have the capacity for adaptation to specific performance evaluation.

Meaningfully designed sets of KPIs have been shown to be successful in collaborative environments (Shi et al. 2014a, Shi et al. 2015). An example of this is the use of email analysis to understand project management performance. For example, analyzing the role of email sentiment (a complex scenario that can be difficult to calculate) during different design phases, and assessing whether the identification of negativity in a team may provide tell-tale signs of impending project delays (Jones et al. 2013). This research utilized communication data, data that is often embodied in abstract form, to evaluate and represent the performance of a project. In this particular case, the abstract data-form proved insightful. Unfortunately, many forms of abstract data are increasingly available to managers. Not all of these will be useful, and those that ultimately are, may not easily reveal their secrets.

Ideally, the process of extracting the KPI from data and producing the visualization display should be facilitated through automation, to reduce the burden of manual processing and intervention. The conceptual model depicted in Figure 8.1 outlines one approach used to capture data automatically, analyze the data and provide KPIs to answer the key questions that project managers and engineers require.

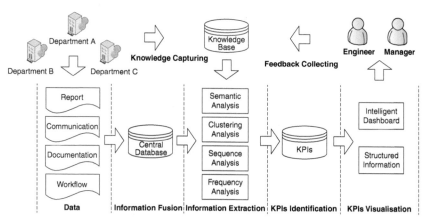

FIGURE 8.1 Conceptual Model for Visual Project Management Support

The model consists of five core steps, namely; Data, Information Fusion, Information Extraction, KPI Identification and KPI Visualization. At its core is the Knowledge Base for the project manager's operating environment.

Step 1—Data Collection

In the first step, identifying the availability and quality of data is essential. This step is also used to evaluate the range of data available as not all data will be used/has been used in the traditional KPI analysis as some data may not be beneficial to the firm. The key objective here is to ascertain what data is available for use, along with the ease of accessing the data.

Step 2—Information Fusion and Knowledge Capture

To increase the accuracy, overcome fragmentation and improve reliability of the information visualization, multiple sources of data should be merged and referenced in order to validate the differing data sources. Knowledge should also be captured from individuals (novice and expert) and project teams in order to shed light on the data that is being extracted. This will give context and domain specific information about any data captured.

Step 3—Information Extraction

This step involves the extraction of data that both include implicit and explicit data patterns, using techniques such as Natural Language Processing (NLP) and Named Entity Recognition (NER).

Step 4—KPI Identification

Next, extracted data patterns are applied to identify and form KPIs. This may include a process of filtering to exclude superfluous data or data with little evidence to suggest that it reveals anything meaningful. KPI identification may also include multiple sources of data. This step may be an iterative process, linking to expert feedback and evaluating the efficacy of automated techniques.

Step 5—KPI Visualization

KPI should be visualized interactively (allowing for browsing, retrieval of selections for comparing and sharing) so that it can adapt to the individual information needs of each project manager or user. This step, as well as the last, is of course entirely emblematic of contemporary discussions of visually supported enacted sensemaking (cf. Bendoly 2016). Throughout the modeling and analysis process, feedback is collected so that the visualization approaches selected adapt in response to the individual users and the feedback they provide. This allows the visualization to provide appropriate fits to questions that may vary and evolve.

8.3   Examination of Use

Consider the application of these steps in the development of a visual dashboard for an international aerospace engineering company.

Step 1—Data Collection

The data collected consisted of 390 In-service projects, occurring between 2012 and 2013. Each project had a number of structured reports associated with it: technical reports, communication documentation and workflow information. Additionally, the project reports contained participant information. Each of the reports contained a number of sub-categories, such as, damage information, assembly part information or repair information. The data were saved and transmitted in multiple formats such as text-based (e.g. .pdf, .doc, .txt etc.), image files (e.g. .jpg, .png etc.) and image-based PDF files. In this case study, we focus on treatment of the text-based information, although the image-based files were also incorporated if they contain meaningful text information. At this stage only raw data was available, which was representative of a workflow and in multiple formats, hence we needed to turn the data into collective information.

Step 2—Information Fusion and Knowledge Capture

Each project and its reports needed to be in a machine-readable form and be classified in terms of their particular features, i.e. represented by a feature vector (such as features of a project—timeframe or project stage). In total, the data set consisted of fifteen unique file types that in principle relate to different project stages and activities. In practice, there is considerable variation from project to project in the rate and time at which the files are generated. Sequencing these file types allows the construction of feature vectors, e.g. stage<planning> → activity<request of information> → data<email>. Based upon these high-level representations, file types can be categorized (see Table 8.1 where Px represents the project number and Tx the proportion of a particular file time). For example, Project 1 had 12 percent of files that were a particular type labeled as T1 (such as .pdf).

In-service projects can involve many collaborators and, as such, each report can involve numerous contributors. Each contributor has agency within the projects:

TABLE 8.1   File-based Feature Vector

	T1	T2	T3	T4	T5	...	T15	Total
P1	0.1212	0	0.2908	0	0.0767	...	0.1153	1
P2	0	0.1132	0.0895	0	0.3004	...	0.0916	1

TABLE 8.2 Transaction-based Feature Vector

	Outgoing	Incoming	Internal	Total
P1	0.3209	0.5356	0.1435	1
P2	0.5030	0.123S	0.3732	1

they assess the situation and take action accordingly. Project managers have very different degrees of control and access to contributors if they are internal or external to their own organization or division. Consequently, they represent different degrees of risk to the project management team. In our work, we view the interactions between separate sources of agency to be a key contributor to overall project complexity.

Our analysis distinguishes between these collaborations by the extent to which they are internal (between company departments and the maintenance teams) or involve external parties (e.g. suppliers, contractors and customers). Files that include evidence of data exchange are thus coded with an additional vector feature (called transaction change). These consist of three types: outgoing, incoming and internal transaction change. Outgoing file types are defined as those sent to clients/contractors outside of the company by internal departments. Incoming file types are those that are received by internal departments by client/contractors. Internal files are those that are sent between organization departments and only circulated between them.

This additional categorization is demonstrated by the summaries in Table 8.2, which shows the relative prevalence of the three categories for each of two In-service projects (P1 and P2). In this example the transactional changes for Project 1 were, 32 percent outgoing, 54 percent incoming and 14 percent internal.

Step 3—Information Extraction

In this case example, the key challenge highlighted was (broadly speaking) the management of and accommodation of operational complexity. In order to have any chance of improving operations, the meaningful codification of complexity was thus critical. This involved generating rules for identifying complexity, as well as the application of those rules and comprehensive analysis to classify projects and to ultimately improve awareness and understanding.

Rule Generation—Complexity Identification

A collection of knowledge-based rules was formulated based on suggestions by senior engineers and through interrogating the data from historical projects, contrasting the balance of frequency between the originator and receiver of project information artifacts. The first of these was that projects with high outgoing but low incoming transactions are considered to have low complexity. In the domain of our case study, these files are mainly damage information and inquiry files from clients or contractors. It is supposed that a relatively small proportion of these arise because the damage is minor and can be extracted from the Standard Repair Manual (SRM) (standard well-documented repair). These projects can be conducted and completed simply and do not require further information requests made to the In-service department.

The second rule was that projects with low outgoing but high incoming transactions are assumed to have high complexity. Multiple requests made by the client/contractor could indicate higher project importance, that the damage is complex to describe or that the customer could not provide sufficient information in the initial project stage. This could mean that the damage is major, the repair process is likely more complex and/or the case is more business critical.

The third rule is that projects with high internal transactions are considered to have high complexity. Aircraft damage complexity will result in an increased level of internal communication. Certain activities will also involve internal communication such as fatigue test reports and stress test reports. These activities are often difficult and time-consuming, involving computational power and complexity, human resources that are highly skilled and physical resources such as specialist equipment. Finally, all other types of projects such as a balanced outgoing/incoming transaction, and low internal transaction are considered to have medium complexity.

Project Clustering

The resulting feature vector categorization derived, leveraging additional transaction data type and subsequent complexity categorizations, is shown in Table 8.3. Captured in this table are 390 In-service projects that are categorized into six clusters. Table 8.3 shows the average outgoing transaction of C1 to be higher than others, while the complexity level of its contained projects (23.85 percent) is low; the average internal transaction of C2 is higher than others, and the complexity level of the contained projects (13.33 percent) is also high; the ratio of outgoing to incoming transactions of C3, C4 and C6 are more balanced.

An alternative depiction of these results is provided in Figures 8.2 and 8.3. In Figure 8.2 we see the projection of feature vectors in a 3-dimensional space (each color indicates an assigned cluster for a plotted project). In Figure 8.3 we see the

TABLE 8.3 Result of Complexity Identification

Cluster	Size	Outgoing (avg.)	Incoming (avg.)	Internal (avg.)	Complexity
C1	93	0.7904	0.1967	0.0129	Low
C2	52	0.5406	0.2194	0.2400	High
C3	95	0.6956	0.2936	0.0108	Medium
C4	30	0.5238	0.4708	0.0054	Medium
C5	47	0.3SS3	0.6056	0.0061	High
C6	73	0.5940	0.3972	0.0088	Medium

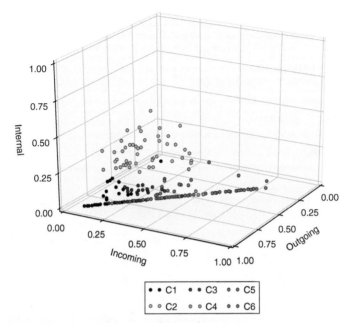

FIGURE 8.2 Visualization of Operational Complexity—I

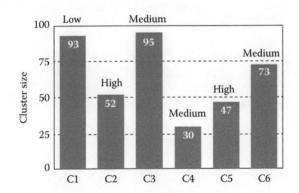

FIGURE 8.3 Visualization of Operational Complexity—II

distribution of cluster size and the assigned complexity level of each cluster. Both of these visualizations provide information that is intended to clarify the nature of communications between interested parties, enabling the project participants to monitor and compare the active/live performance of projects.

Steps 4–5—KPI Identification and Visualization

Engineers and project managers working in the In-service maintenance department are often committed to multiple projects concurrently. It is essential for those managers to understand the execution status and performance level of individual projects, and then allocate resources accordingly, in order to maximize the project output. This is a key element of managing the capability of their project teams. Project managers need to consider multiple KPIs against multiple projects, against the expertise at their disposal so that projects do not overrun in timescale. The integration of multiple KPIs across many projects and analyzing and visualizing the complexity of any project is key when identifying potential delays.

Figure 8.4 shows an example dashboard that integrates multiple KPIs that are used to facilitate comparative analysis against KPI-4 (project complexity). The KPIs shown in Figure 8.4 were chosen because they were the most salient features

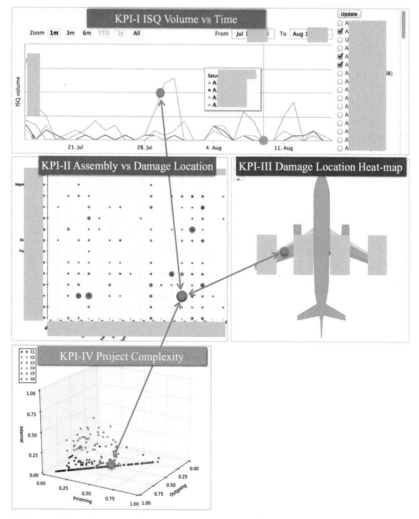

FIGURE 8.4 Visualization of Integrated KPIs: An Intelligent Dashboard

in relation to complexity that could be analyzed by project managers comparatively against the KPI-4, discussed in Steps 1–3. The other visual KPIs include: KPI-1: In-Service Query (ISQ) volume vs time; KPI-2: Assembly vs damage location; and KPI-3: Heat map of damage locations. KPI-1 enables project managers to review current workload to be distributed across the team, as well as the detailed information and related aircraft types; KPI-2 allows project managers to assess the difficulties and workload required for each individual project by examining its damage location(s), severity and assembly parts with the size of each dot representing the frequency of the damage type; KPI-3 enables project managers to have a comprehensive understanding of the damage location and frequency for particular aircraft types. It is self-evident that the combination of these KPIs allows project managers to be more informed when allocating time, people and other resources when considering the complexity of a project. With additional complexity information about each project based on intelligent clustering algorithms, it is arguable that project managers could dynamically adjust the workplan and resource allocation to more appropriately respond to project changes in conditions and circumstances.

8.4   Lessons for Future Development

To discuss the visualization of complex data we ask the question whether the data displayed has the "right stuff" for project managers in global engineering firms. The term "right stuff" is a familiar one in the aerospace industry. It was first coined in the book of the same name by Tom Wolfe (1979) and was used to describe US test pilots and the first astronauts selected for the NASA space program. The test pilots were chosen because they were considered to have the right combination of mental and physical attributes—"the right stuff," to undertake the task successfully. In a form of critical retrospection, let us now consider whether the dashboard in our case example was in fact a fit to operational needs.

Reflections from the project managers on the visualization of complex KPIs can be grouped into themes, identifying reoccurring ideas and recommendation patterns—a standardized way of presenting feedback data (Burnard et al. 2008). Three main themes emerged regarding the utility of dashboards incorporating aspects of project complexity: (a) the right time: access, efficiency and productivity; (b) the right information: granularity and dimensionality of information; (c) the right way: implementation considerations for a large global company.

The Right Time

The visual representation of KPI provided novel opportunities to improve productivity by reducing access barriers, facilitating comprehension and enhancing decision making informed by In-service documentation. At present, current engineering design documentation can be extensive, time-consuming and complex to access. Project managers reported factors such as frequent interruptions and poor text layout, with documents often containing hyperlinks. The dashboard provides a much more efficient mechanism for information processing. The appreciation of large volumes of data could now occur holistically with much greater ease in the system of idioms developed, than through any pure text representation.

In relation to decision making, the In-service department dealt with high time pressure constraints, often needing to make decisions and provide services within an eight-hour turn-around period. The ability to gauge the complexity of a repair task enables managers to better forecast project completion dates. This capability is core to their customer base, with visualizations and fused information decreasing decision-making process time in comparison to reading In-service documentation.

The Right Information

A second key theme that emerged was the dashboard's ability to show the user the appropriate granularity, or level of detail, of relevant information. A visualization of complex data requires the capability to drill down in detail. For instance, an overall picture of the aircraft highlighting damage was not as useful as a detailed image of the damage location, particularly when the size of the image on the layout (the size of each dot in Figure 8.4, KPI-2, indicating the frequency of a damage type) is presented as an indication of severity.

To be sure, the right dashboard content should not simply be a rehashing of common knowledge for the user. It should provide informative content in a familiar manner that matches the visual dialect of users. It should allow for interactivity such that confirmation of familiar content can be provided, but it should also permit exploration that can facilitate further sensemaking. Therefore, we propose the following statement to be relevant broadly to dashboard designs:

> The most effective dashboards visualize data by means of default granularity levels that fit the task-specific needs of the user, while providing customization options that can confirm contextual knowledge and extend beyond it.

The Right Way

The dashboard for the In-service department was designed to convey complexity in a way most easily understood, and in turn capable of facilitating decision making. However, that process of deploying dashboards within the department was not free of its own complexities. First, the ability to maintain data integrity is a major consideration and this should be based on relevant key decision data particular to the department. In support of planned on-going use, rigorous procedures would need to be in place to ensure that key decision data was maintained. In order to enable automatic extraction, information would need to be available in an extractable digital format.

Although these considerations are context-specific in reference to the case study site, implementation procedures could be put into place to allow the dashboard to be applied to the whole organization and other organizations. SRM documentation, for example, is a prominent area that has a vast dataset where suitable icons could be developed to represent the individual SRM documents in a dashboard summary format with an aim to increase productivity.

Performance evaluation in engineering projects like the In-service department of a global aerospace company is becoming increasingly challenging. Operational processes are becoming more complex, the volume of requests is increasing, resources are more distributed and collaborations are increasing with a network of external organizations. The dashboard discussed in this chapter provided visual support for repair operations based on the use and design of KPIs to evaluate a complex set of data and contexts, in order that project managers gain a better understanding of any project execution status, project efficiency and resource allocation.

Acknowledgements

The research reported in this chapter is funded by Engineering and Physical Sciences Research Council (EP/K014196/1). The authors would like to thank the industrial collaborators and their engineers for their input and support on this project.

References

Atkinson, R. 1999. Project management: cost, time and quality, two best guesses and a phenomenon, its time to accept other success criteria. *International Journal of Project Management* 17(6): 337–342.

Bendoly, E. 2014. Systems dynamics understanding in project execution: information sharing quality and psychological safety. *Production and Operations Management* 23(8): 1352–1369.

Bendoly, E. 2016. Fit, bias and enacted sensemaking in data visualization: frameworks for continuous development in operations and supply chain management analytics. *Journal of Business Logistics* 37(1): 6–17.

Bititci, U., Garengo, P., Dörfler, V. and Nudurupati, S. 2012. Performance measurement: Challenges for tomorrow. *International Journal of Management Reviews* 14(3): 305–327.

Bryde, D.J. 2005. Methods for managing different perspectives of project success. *British Journal of Management* 16(2): 119–131.

Burnard, P., Gill, P., Stewart, K., Treasure E. and Chadwick, B. 2008. Analysing and presenting qualitative data. *British Dental Journal* 204(8): 429–432.

Carey, E., Culley, S. and Weber, F. 2013. Establishing key elements for handling in-service information and knowledge, in *The 19th International Conference on Engineering Design, ICED13*: Seoul, South Korea.

Chan, A.P. and Chan, A.P. 2004. Key performance indicators for measuring construction success. *Benchmarking: An International Journal* 11(2): 203–221.

Hicks, B. 2013. The language of collaborative engineering projects, in *19th International Conference on Engineering Design, ICED13*: Seoul, South Korea.

Jones, S., Payne, S., Hicks, B. and Watts, L., 2013. Visualization of heterogeneous text data in collaborative engineering projects, in *The 3rd IEEE Workshop on Interactive Visual Text Analytics*: Atlanta, GA.

Lauras, M., Marques, G. and Gourc, D. 2010. Towards a multi-dimensional project performance measurement system. *Decision Support Systems* 48(2): 342–353.

Parmenter, D. 2010. *Key performance indicators (KPI): developing, implementing, and using winning KPIs*. Hoboken, NJ New York: John Wiley & Sons.

Pheng, L.S. and Chuan, Q.T. 2006. Environmental factors and work performance of project managers in the construction industry. *International Journal of Project Management* 24(1): 24–37.

Shi, L., Gopsill, J., Newnes, L. and Culley, S. 2014a. A sequence-based approach to analysing and representing engineering project normality, in ICTAI 2014: *26th IEEE International Conference on Tools with Artificial Intelligence*: Limassol, Cyprus.

Shi, L., Newnes, L., Culley, S. and Hicks, B. 2014b. Predicting the performance of collaborative manufacturing projects: knowledge discovery from digital assets, in *3rd Annual EPSRC Manufacturing the Future Conference*: Glasgow, United Kingdom.

Shi, L., Newnes, L., Culley, S., Gopsill, J., Jones, S. and Snider, C. 2015. Identifying and visualising KPIs for collaborative engineering projects: a knowledge-based approach. *International Conference on Engineering Design, ICED 15*. 27–30 July 2015: Politecnico Di Milano, Italy.

Toor, S.-u.-R. and Ogunlana, S.O. 2010. Beyond the "iron triangle": stakeholder perception of key performance indicators (KPIs) for large-scale public sector development projects. *International Journal of Project Management* 28(3): 228–236.

Wolfe, T. 1979. *The right stuff*. New York: Farrar, Straus and Giroux.

Xie, Y., Culley, S. and Weber, F. 2011. Applying context to organize unstructured information in aerospace industry, in *18th International Conference on Engineering Design, ICED 11*: Copenhagen, Denmark.

9

ELECTRONIC HEALTH RECORD-BASED VISUALIZATION TOOLS

Randi Foraker

Electronic health records are used to manage patient demographic and clinical data. Many such platforms also assist healthcare systems with scheduling appointments, and can facilitate the billing of insurance companies and patients for services rendered. The underlying functional objective of electronic health record systems is therefore to enable the entry, storage, and access of patient data by healthcare providers and health system employees. The promise of electronic health records is that their use increases healthcare system efficiency and healthcare quality, and their data can be used for population health management at the health system level. While the transition from paper medical charting to electronic health record systems has positively impacted healthcare delivery in terms of faster appointment scheduling and relatively seamless billing procedures, this chapter describes a data visualization solution to one of their inherent drawbacks: notably their limited interactive capabilities, which can negatively affect the patient–healthcare provider encounter.

During a clinical encounter, healthcare providers have a finite amount of time to allocate to each patient. Compounding this problem is the fact that electronic health record data are typically stored in discrete fields on different screens throughout the system, as a result individual data points—laboratory values, biometric readings, medical history, patient demographics, and medication lists—remain siloed from one another within the system. Unfortunately, commercially available electronic health record platforms provide few, if any, built-in data visualization tools to make the information stored therein useful and easily digestible for patient care. Due to these shortcomings, the electronic health record tends to serve predominantly as a passive data-collection system, and healthcare providers spend the majority of the clinical encounter searching for and entering data relevant to the patient's care rather than interacting with the patient (Street et al., 2014). Adding data visualization capabilities to existing electronic health record systems allows for more efficient use of the data repository and enhances communication at the point-of-care between the patient and healthcare provider.

9.1 Appreciating the Audience and Context

Although some patients see their healthcare providers for annual physicals or "well-visits," many encounters involve acute problems that the patient wants resolved by their healthcare provider during that visit. Patients generally see their healthcare providers as experts who are trusted to treat disease and manage health. Healthcare providers are problem-solvers, and a majority of their time is dedicated to deciphering data clues in order to deliver high-quality guideline-based care for curing and preventing disease. In addition to providing treatment for acute and chronic healthcare issues, healthcare providers are tasked with distilling down a large amount of patient-level data to educate patients on the most salient aspects of disease management and assist them in reaching their health goals. Truly, healthcare providers can be highly influential at the point-of-care in eliciting changes in patient behavior. Health promotion discussions that are delivered by healthcare providers tend to show success; even brief smoking cessation sessions are effective, and United States Public Health Service guidelines recommend all healthcare providers consult patients who smoke (Fiore et al., 2008). Along with these many responsibilities, healthcare providers often have back-to-back appointments scheduled throughout the day to attend to multiple patients with diverse needs.

In this context, the healthcare provider does not wish to have their workflow interrupted or be distracted from the task at hand. To make their day's work more efficient, many providers use clinical decision support systems, available in commercial electronic health record platforms, to deliver healthcare reminders (i.e. when vaccinations or cancer screenings are due) and alert to possible errors (i.e. potentially harmful drug interactions or duplicate laboratory orders). Evidence suggests that clinical decision support systems change healthcare provider behavior, increase adherence to clinical guidelines, and moreover are acceptable to providers (Rothman et al., 2012). These reminders and alerts however are typically presented as "pop-up" text messages on the provider's computer screen, lacking interactivity. Such messages are designed exclusively for an audience of healthcare providers, and often do not prompt discussion with patients.

Meanwhile, patients are increasingly aware of certain aspects of their own health; a growing number of patients use activity trackers and calorie counters on their mobile devices, and many seek medical information online (Fox et al., 2013). Across our society, there is an increasing focus on quantifying our lives: from the steps we take to the foods we eat (*The Economist*, 2012). Concurrent to these data points collected by patients in the real world, there is an increasing emphasis on "personalized medicine" in the healthcare setting—healthcare that is tailored to the genomic and clinical data comprising the individual patient. Given that patients and healthcare providers are often savvy consumers of technology and

FIGURE 9.1 Data Entry, Storage, and Visualization in the Electronic Health Record

data (see http://iianalytics.com/research/value-added-data-visualization, accessed December 15, 2015), who are avid users of mobile health applications and wearable devices outside of the clinic, electronic health record systems are remarkably void of interactive features for bringing these data to life. There exists great potential for interactive healthcare data visualizations, if designed with the end-users in mind, to enhance patient–provider communication about health and overcome numeracy and health literacy challenges at the point-of-care (Figure 9.1).

With this in mind, a research team at a large Midwestern medical center initiated the design, development, and implementation of an interactive, easy-to-use, electronic health record-based clinical decision support system for use in primary care. The point-of-care web application, called Stroke Prevention in Healthcare Delivery Environments (SPHERE), automatically populates with the patient's electronic health record data (inputs) and provides a tailored health profile visualization (outputs) nested within the electronic health record. SPHERE was developed by an interdisciplinary team representing public health, biomedical informatics, and internal medicine to allow patients and healthcare providers to view and interact with the patient's risk factors for cardiovascular disease to see how favorable changes in the risk profile would translate to better overall health.

9.2   Design Principles Applied

SPHERE presents to the provider within the electronic health record as a text-based clinical decision support system alert. When the clinical decision support alert is clicked, it triggers existing application programming interfaces (APIs) which collect current encounter-level clinical data for the patient from the electronic health record vendor's live database, and delivers them to the SPHERE application via a secure POST http request. The SPHERE application then retrieves historical clinical data from the Enterprise Data Warehouse (EDW), a data repository of all clinical data from within the healthcare system, and renders an individualized risk profiling and visualization on an embedded instance of a web browser engine (Foraker et al., 2015a). Only the most contemporary data are displayed in the visualization, streamlining otherwise multiple longitudinal data points into a lean and simple representation for ease of interpretation by the audience.

The science behind SPHERE is an evidence-based cardiovascular health algorithm (Lloyd-Jones et al., 2010). SPHERE leverages the algorithm to classify seven behaviors and factors into categories of *ideal* (2 points), *intermediate* (1 point), and *poor* (0 points) and calculates and presents a cardiovascular health score in real-time (Figure 9.2). Each SPHERE component is modifiable by actions of the healthcare provider or the patient. Traditionally, these components are referred to as "risk" factors instead of being recognized as opportunities for improvement. Indeed, worse overall cardiovascular health scores have been associated with myriad adverse health outcomes, including heart disease, cancer, and stroke. Framing an overall cardiovascular score in terms of "health"—summing points across all behaviors and factors, dividing by the total possible (14 points), and multiplying by 100—discourages the audience from conceptualizing each input as an opportunity for "loss aversion."

SPHERE uses color-coded visual-analog scales to indicate ideal (green), intermediate (yellow), and poor (red) categories of cardiovascular disease risk. At the top of the SPHERE application, the overall cardiovascular health score is presented

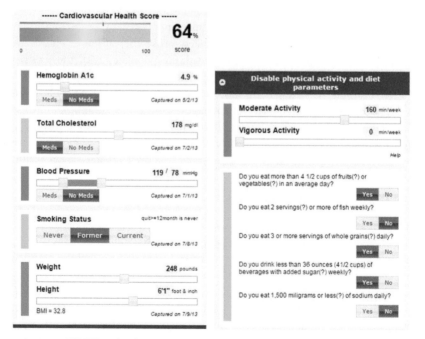

FIGURE 9.2 SPHERE Application

along a color continuum ranging from 0 percent (worst, red) to 100 percent (best, green). SPHERE's color-coding schema is intuitive, and allows healthcare providers to quickly identify patients at high, medium, and low cardiovascular risk and to assess the *comprehensive* cardiovascular health of the patient. Similarly, utilizing the stoplight color scheme translates complex health data for the patient and clearly presents which behaviors they should "stop" doing, proceed with "caution" when doing, and to "go" ahead and keep doing. Color-coding, such as that used in SPHERE, has enhanced patients' understanding of health data—especially among those with low numeracy skills (Oettinger et al., 2009). It is therefore characteristic of the interest in fitting audience/task needs with visual artifact design (Bendoly 2016; and Chapter 3).

Another design characteristic of the SPHERE application is the presentation of cardiovascular health information within a single panel. Gestalt groupings of data elements organize the application into laboratory values (hemoglobin A1c and total cholesterol), up-to-date clinical data (blood pressure, smoking status, and body mass index), and health behaviors (physical activity and diet). Five behaviors and factors (body mass index, blood pressure, smoking status, hemoglobin A1c, and total cholesterol) are collected during usual clinical care, and are almost always available in the electronic health record in a primary care setting. Therefore, those risk factors are presented at the top of the SPHERE application and screen scrolling is minimized. As physical activity and diet data are not typically recorded in the electronic health record, these two risk factors are contained in an expandable section of the application and must be manually entered at the point-of-care. However, the application—including the algorithm and visualization—will run with or without the latter two health behaviors.

SPHERE's streamlined algorithm and resulting data visualization contains seven individual data elements and one overall cardiovascular health score, which serves to minimize data overload as discussed in Chapter 2. In the case of missing data (and threats outlined in Chapter 1), the overall cardiovascular health score is calculated from the total possible points according to the data that are available. This design element allows for the audience to assess the picture of the patient's health and to make healthcare decisions given the available data at the point-of-care. In this way, the SPHERE application helps the audience make sense of the data—which are otherwise stored in different areas of the electronic health record—and is responsive to the time constraints of a typical healthcare encounter.

Importantly, SPHERE is not a static visualization—while the visualization is anchored on the patient's current biometric and behavioral values, SPHERE is designed as a responsive web application and updates its visualization automatically with each update to the data. Dynamic design elements of the application include slider bars and buttons for each cardiovascular health input to allow the healthcare provider to interact with the visualization to show the patient how each of the variables can be changed to impact their overall cardiovascular health output. Such highly personalized inputs allow the patient to see the cause–effect

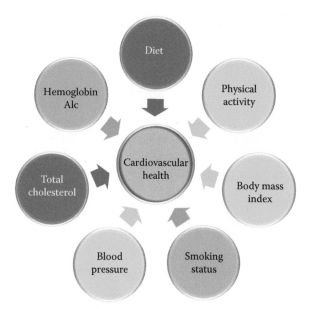

FIGURE 9.3 Conceptual Relationship Between SPHERE Inputs and Outputs

relationship between each risk factor and the outcome. The interactive feature aids what healthcare experts call "shared decision-making," and in this text is referred to as "sensemaking," where healthcare providers and patients collaborate to discuss treatment and referral options for cardiovascular disease risk management.

Manipulation of an input on the SPHERE interface shows the independent cause–effect relationship between that specific risk factor and the overall cardiovascular health score: if weight changes from "red" to "yellow," the overall cardiovascular health score will increase by a pre-specified amount (Figure 9.3). A limitation of the underlying evidence-based algorithm is that it does not capture the complex causal dependencies between each of the inputs. For example, weight loss from "red" to "yellow" may also in turn decrease blood pressure and fasting glucose toward favorable levels. However, the underlying algorithm and SPHERE interface require these inputs be adjusted independently. Considering the audience and the time constraints of a clinical encounter, it may be preferable to provide data in terms of these simple, independent associations rather than in terms of their complex causal relationships.

9.3 Examination of Use

Usability assessments can be used to enhance electronic health record-based applications for specific audiences. As usability factors pose one of the major obstacles to health information technology adoption, it is essential to consider usability at the early stage of the system development life cycle. Deploying an audience-centered design should include a needs assessment as well as iterative end-user usability testing. A unified framework of electronic health record usability design and development—the Tasks, Users, Representations, and Functions (TURF) theory—is commonly used to evaluate electronic health records (Zhang et al., 2011). The same evaluation methods can be used in the design and testing phases of electronic health record-based visualization applications.

The TURF theory can be applied to electronic health record-based visualizations as follows. Members of a clinical advisory group, comprising healthcare providers and patient focus group members (*Users*), are invited to express their needs, which inform the application's design. Users are asked to describe their method of usual care (*Tasks*) and the data they require or expect (*Representations*) during the process of a clinical care encounter. Once a visualization application prototype is created from the TURF process described above, a series of end-user think-aloud protocol assessments should be conducted with the clinical advisory group to identify usability problems for further application refinement for that particular audience. Think-aloud assessments can be conducted by giving the application to the healthcare provider or patient and asking them to "think-aloud" as they explore its functionality (*Functions*) as if they were using the application during a healthcare encounter. The think-aloud assessment can help designers identify aspects of the application that are not yet intuitive to the intended audience and must be modified.

However, beyond subjective usability considerations, perhaps more salient are objective measures of impacts on actual behavior. To assess the effect of SPHERE on patient's risk factors for stroke over a one-year period, SPHERE was launched in the study's intervention clinic, and data were collected from the intervention clinic and from a clinic that did not have access to SPHERE—the control clinic (Figure 9.4). On average, the dose of the intervention was under three minutes, and over a one-year period there were 390 SPHERE views for 410 eligible patients. In the clinic with access to SPHERE, the proportion of obese patients decreased from 47 percent to 43 percent, and the proportion of normal-weight patients increased from 15 percent to 19 percent over a one-year period (average weight loss: 2.7 kg). Diabetes status also changed favorably in the intervention clinic: the proportion of patients without diabetes increased from 57 percent to 63 percent over the one-year period. These same metrics either stayed the same or worsened in the control clinic (Foraker et al., 2015b).

Healthcare providers reported high usability and acceptability of the SPHERE application on the domains of content, accuracy, format, ease of use, and timeliness. After using the SPHERE application for a one-year period, healthcare providers responded to survey questions using a 5-point Likert scale: 1 = Never/Almost Never and 5 = Always/Almost Always. Accuracy scored the highest with an average of 4.3 + 0.6; while content scored lowest at an average of 3.8 + 0.9. One provider scored the SPHERE application low on all domains, which may indicate one individual's dissatisfaction with technology rather than a critique of SPHERE in particular. SPHERE researchers concluded that the application

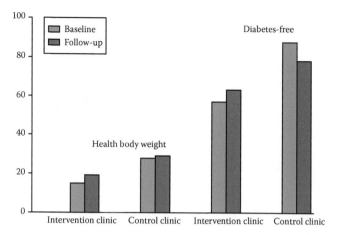

FIGURE 9.4 One-year Changes in the SPHERE Intervention Clinic and Control Clinic

served to improve patient care, enhance patient–healthcare provider communication, and optimize the utility of the electronic health record for patients and healthcare providers.

9.4   Lessons for Future Development

Point-of-care applications such as SPHERE seek to transform healthcare and improve patients' health by delivering the *right data* (cardiovascular health score) to the *right people* (patients and healthcare providers) at the *right time* (during the healthcare encounter). This integrative, workflow-aware, and user-friendly approach to data visualization makes the electronic health record an active part of such patient–healthcare provider dialogues, as opposed to serving as a passive information capture tool as is commonly the case. The power of visualizations in healthcare is that disparate, complex data can be communicated quickly and concisely to a variety of audiences. In a 15-minute clinical encounter, healthcare providers do not have the time to hunt across multiple screens for the data they need to construct a risk score for the patient. However, if the data are automatically collated and presented in a simple visualization, the provider can easily risk-stratify the patient and decide what advice or treatment to offer them.

Much of the data entry and retrieval during the clinical encounter is done with the computer screen turned away from the patient, failing to involve the patient in their own healthcare. Critical to quality healthcare delivery is patient-centered care, which engages the patient in shared decision-making regarding disease management and treatment. Applications such as SPHERE require the computer screen to be turned toward the patient, enhancing patient–healthcare provider communication. A benefit of using data visualization in the communication process is to enhance patient understanding of important concepts. Data visualizations can empower patients to manage their health conditions effectively, and can help patients with low health literacy better understand their illness (Faisal et al., 2013).

Electronic health record-integrated visualization applications have the potential to improve the quality of patient care. Extant evidence demonstrates improved patient outcomes through implementation of clinical informatics tools—without visualization features—in domains of medicine spanning infectious disease, surgery, and chronic disease. The success of such tools is traced to increased provider adherence to clinical guidelines and Institute of Medicine recommendations for appropriate referrals and treatments. Adding visualization and interactive features to other existing clinical informatics applications would likely improve the quality of care and patient outcomes, regardless of the healthcare setting or disease of interest.

The SPHERE application was designed to be easily implemented into clinical practice and widely disseminated. It is currently operating within Epic, one of the most commonly used electronic health record systems in the United States, and the application was built to interoperate with a variety of electronic health record platforms. SPHERE was programmed to integrate seamlessly into provider workflow, thus differentiating itself from other electronic health record-based clinical decision support systems.

Critical to SPHERE's success from a healthcare provider perspective was its ease of use, timeliness, and non–obtrusive design. Healthcare providers found the interactive features of the visualization to be intuitive. These same features helped to guide conversations with patients about disease prevention and treatment. Data were delivered to the application and presented in the SPHERE visualization within seconds, precluding a time-intensive manual search throughout the electronic health record for the necessary data elements. To improve the timeliness of the application, SPHERE was launched when the healthcare provider navigated to the order screen in the electronic health record. This meant that the healthcare provider was positioned to order a laboratory test if a data element, such as hemoglobin A1c or total cholesterol, was missing from the SPHERE application. At this point the healthcare provider can discuss with the patient whether to prescribe a medication to control one of the health factors shown in red on the application. In addition, the SPHERE visualization was presented asynchronously in a panel along the right-hand side of the electronic medical record screen. This allowed the healthcare provider to navigate around the electronic health record as usual, and their typical workflow was not interrupted.

It must be acknowledged that cutting-edge visualization capabilities may be limited by features of the electronic medical record platform itself. While many of the major electronic health record platforms have built-in web application functionality, development of responsive web applications is often limited by the generation of web browser supported by the parent platform. As a result, features of visualizations and the quality of the renderings may be a few generations behind what is currently available to mobile application users outside of the clinic.

A common theme SPHERE's research team heard from patients and healthcare providers is that patients should have access to their health data outside of the clinical encounter. Patients want to be able to manage their risk factors and explore data visualizations at home, on their computer or mobile device. Data security and patient privacy preclude the automatic integration of patient data with web applications on home computers or mobile devices. Patient health information stored within electronic health records is considered private, and is protected by the Health Insurance Portability and Accountability Act (HIPAA) that was passed by Congress in 1996 (HIPAA, 1996).

Under the HIPAA Privacy Rule, a federal law, patients have the right to request access to their medical and billing record (78 Fed. Reg.). However, there are still restrictions on how electronic health record data can be transmitted. Specifically, patient demographic and clinical data remain behind the healthcare system's firewall unless an externally facing, secure personal health record platform is supported and maintained by the health system. And even then, only certain data are passed securely to patient-facing personal health record platforms, which effectively limit the use of health data visualizations to the context of the clinical encounter.

Despite these limitations, the promise of data visualization in healthcare delivery is to facilitate the prevention and management of disease in populations of patients for who shared decision-making is paramount. Applications like SPHERE should be designed with a generalizable framework in mind, as electronic health record-integrated visualization tools have broad application to clinical decision-making and disease prevention and management. Current best practices can be applied in the development of visualizations that incorporate risk factors for a variety of health conditions to reach patients in diverse healthcare settings. Design principles will continue to evolve with the changing healthcare and consumer landscape. Critical to this evolution will be changes in policy regarding data security to allow for patient access to their personalized data visualizations beyond the point of care.

References

78 Fed. Reg. 5566-5702 (Jan. 25, 2013), amending 45 C.F.R. Parts 160, 164.
Bendoly, E. 2016. Fit, bias and enacted sensemaking in data visualization: frameworks for continuous in operations and supply chain management analytics. *Journal of Business Logistics* 37(1): 6–17.
Editorial Staff. 2012. Counting every moment. *The Economist*, March 3, 2012.
Faisal S, Blandford A, Potts HW. 2013. Making sense of personal health information: challenges for information visualization. *Health Informatics Journal* 19(3):198–217.
Fiore MC, Jaén CR, Baker TB, Bailey, W., Benowitz, N., Curry, S., Dorfman, S., Froelicher, E., Goldstein, M., Healton, C., Henderson, P., Heyman, R., Koh, H., Kottke, T., Lando, H., Mecklenburg, R., Memelstein, R., Mullen, P., Orleans, T., Robinson, L., Stitzer, M., Tommasello, A., Villego, L., Wewers, M.E. 2008. Treating tobacco use and dependence:

2008 update. Clinical Practice Guideline. Rockville, MD: US Department of Health and Human Services. Public Health Service, May.

Foraker RE, Kite B, Kelley MM, Lai AM, Roth C, Lopetegui MA, Shoben AB, Langan M, Rutledge NL, Payne PR. 2015a. EHR-based visualization tool: adoption rates, satisfaction, and patient outcomes. *EGEMS (Washington, DC)* 3(2): 1159.

Foraker RE, Shoben AB, Lai AM, Payne PR, Kelley M, Lopetegui MA, Langan M, Tindle HA, Jackson RD. 2015b. Electronic health record-based assessment of cardiovascular health. *Circulation* 131: AMP12.

Fox S, Duggan M. 2013. Health Online. Washington, DC: Pew Internet & American Life; January 15, www.pewinternet.org/Reports/2013/Health-online/Summary-of-Findings.aspx [accessed December 21, 2015].

Lloyd-Jones DM, Hong Y, Labarthe D, Mozaffarian D, Appel LJ, Van Horn L. 2010. Defining and setting national goals for cardiovascular health promotion and disease reduction. *Circulation* 121(4): 586–613.

Oettinger MD, Finkle JP, Esserman D, Whitehead L, Spain TK, Pattishall SR, Rothman RL, Perrin EM. 2009. Color-coding improves parental understanding of body mass index charting. *Academic Pediatrics* 9(5): 330–338.

Rothman B, Leonard JC, Vigoda MM. 2012. Future of electronic health records: implications for decision support. *Mount Sinai Journal of Medicine*, 79(6): 757–768.

Street RL Jr, Liu L, Farber NJ, Chen Y, Calvitti A, Zuest D, Gabuzda MT, Bell K, Gray B, Rick S, Ashfaq S, Agha Z. 2014. Provider interaction with the electronic health record: the effects on patient-centered communication in medical encounters. *Patient Education and Counselling* 96(3): 315–319.

The Health Insurance Portability and Accountability Act of 1996 (HIPAA). P.L. No. 104–191, 110 Stat. 1938 (1996).

Zhang J, Walji MF. 2011. TURF: toward a unified framework of EHR usability. *Journal of Biomedical Informatics* 44(6): 1056–1067.

10

OPTIMIZATION, VISUALIZATION AND DATA MAPPING FOR HVAC PRODUCT DISTRIBUTION

James W. Hamister, Michael J. Magazine and George G. Polak

The 2J Supply Company, Inc. is a major wholesale distributor of heating, ventilating and air conditioning (HVAC) products in the Midwest and Greater Ohio Valley. A privately held business, 2J Supply was founded over 50 years ago and is headquartered in Dayton, Ohio with nine distribution centers located in Ohio, Kentucky and West Virginia. 2J carries a full line of commercial HVAC equipment and supplies, listing 8,000 available SKUs. The firm sells primarily to HVAC contractors, and is positioned as a high-service provider, with job-site delivery to large-volume customers providing a distinctive market advantage. To date, 2J has relied on internally developed distribution management software. However, the firm has grown rapidly in recent years, and management has decided to consider a pilot project that would assess the value proposition represented by an investment in data analytics capabilities.

Working in partnership with 2J, we proposed a comprehensive solution to achieve the project's goals. Illustrated in Figure 10.1, the effort included abstract modeling, populating the models with realistic data extractions, coding applied to low-cost, readily available tools, and manager-friendly implementation in the field. For this project a mathematical programming model was translated into the Microsoft Visual Basic for Applications (VBA) computer programming language implemented within Microsoft Excel. In turn, VBA commands required translation via an application programming interface (API) into statements in the syntax of the Open Solver Excel add-in (Mason 2012). Appropriate VBA input/output functions allowed the solution given by Open Solver to be formatted in tabular form, which was in turn translated into informative and visually appealing geographical maps. Finally, the visual output required English language descriptions in a business vernacular. Together, these activities transform raw data into potential actions, the process known as sensemaking that is discussed in detail in Chapter 1 of this text.

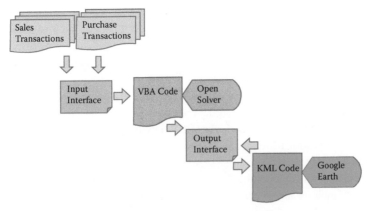

FIGURE 10.1 Process Overview

10.1 Appreciating the Audience and Context

2J Supply has broad leverage over supply chain costs in its regional industrial role. The deterministic cost minimization model presented in Hamister et al. (2016) integrated sourcing, order lot sizing and immediate downstream distribution decisions in a single formulation in order to enhance this advantage. The model design avoided the suboptimization inherent in treating these variables separately. The result was a concave and nonseparable objective function, but a sophisticated approach of decomposition and bounding allowed for effective heuristic solution generation. Even large mathematical programming models are amenable to solutions by widely available software, including the Open Solver add-in for Microsoft Excel.

For the pilot study we considered the Freon family of products given its fairly well-defined selling season, its sourcing from multiple suppliers and its fairly steady sales rate. These characteristics fit the assumptions of our model and made interpretation of our findings straightforward. All purchasing and sales transactions for 2013 for two Freon part numbers were extracted to .csv files (R22 representing 52.5 percent of unit sales and R410A representing 47.5 percent; from seven sources, nine DCs and 750 customers). We used a pivot table to extract sales per month to verify high-demand season. April through July mark the high-demand season for Freon.

Next we prepared the data for input to the Open Solver. The first step in this process was to determine purchase quantities per supplier. In practice, purchase and sales quantities are not likely to be exactly equal for the same time period, and thus to balance purchasing and sales we calculated percentage buy from each supplier and applied that percentage to total units sold. We also had to estimate unit transportation costs. This task required identification of the inventory (DC) nodes and location information for each DC on a separate worksheet of an Excel workbook using a user-defined function

(UDF) to extract the latitude and longitude from an address. Customer node information was then developed, using another UDF adapted from Bendoly (2013), to identify geographic information for each node. This function uses address information to determine latitude and longitude (geocode) values for each location.

Holding costs were applied at each DC node, at 24 percent per year for four months of product family cost. Logistics costs were separately calculated for inbound and outbound lanes. The inbound cost of 1.1 cents/mile was based on skid-quantity quotes for hazardous materials including Freon. Outbound costs were estimated based on a truck operating cost of $1.045 per mile, a labor cost of $23 per hour for two people, Freon representing 20 percent of the delivery, and a 20 mph average travel rate, resulting in 8.8 cents/mile unit delivery cost. The fixed order cost was estimated at $50 from direct labor cost at $23/hour with two employees, lease cost for the delivery truck, and the purchasing agent's time. The validity of these estimates for parameters was confirmed by the supply chain manager at 2J.

Once the workbook was populated with data, coded routines were written by us in VBA for Excel called the Open Solver to find and report an approximately optimal solution. The routine below creates an initial optimization model, employing functions included in the Open Solver API (Mason 2012, 2016).

```
Sub Model_Creation(CompSheet As Worksheet, num_sources,
num_Dcs, num_customers)

    OpenSolver.ResetModel Sheet:=CompSheet

' --- Objective Definition
    OpenSolver.SetObjectiveFunctionCell CompSheet.Cells(3,
    35), Sheet:=CompSheet
    OpenSolver.SetObjectiveSense MinimiseObjective,
    Sheet:=CompSheet

' --- Variables Definition
    OpenSolver.SetDecisionVariables Union(CompSheet.
    Range(Cells(26, 14), Cells(26, 14 + num_Dcs - 1)), _
    CompSheet.Range(Cells(39, 14),
    Cells(39 + num_sources - 1, 14 + num_Dcs - 1)), _
    CompSheet.Range(Cells(49, 34), Cells(49 + num_Dcs - 1,
    34 + num_customers - 1))), Sheet:=CompSheet

' --- Constraints Definition
    ' Flow conservation at DCs
    OpenSolver.AddConstraint CompSheet.Range(Cells(69, 14),
    Cells(69, 14 + num_Dcs - 1)), RelationEQ, _ CompSheet.
    Range(Cells(70, 14), Cells(70, 14 + num_Dcs - 1)),
    Sheet:=CompSheet
```

```
' Satisfying demand at customers
OpenSolver.AddConstraint CompSheet.Range(Cells(69, 34),
Cells(69, 34 + num_customers - 1)), RelationEQ, _
CompSheet.Range(Cells(30, 34), Cells(30, 34 + num_
customers - 1)), Sheet:=CompSheet

' Satisfying supply constraints at sources
OpenSolver.AddConstraint CompSheet.Range(Cells(39, 2),
Cells(39 + num_sources - 1, 2)), _
RelationEQ, CompSheet.Range(Cells(4, 1), Cells(4 + num_
sources - 1, 1)), Sheet:=CompSheet

' Elementary Analysis Cut
OpenSolver.AddConstraint CompSheet.Range(Cells(26, 14),
Cells(26, 14 + num_Dcs - 1)), RelationGE, _ CompSheet.
Range(Cells(27, 14), Cells(27, 14 + num_Dcs - 1)),
Sheet:=CompSheet

' Jensen's Inequality Cut
OpenSolver.AddConstraint CompSheet.Range(Cells(26, 14),
Cells(26, 14 + num_Dcs - 1)), RelationGE, _ CompSheet.
Range(Cells(28, 14), Cells(28, 14 + num_Dcs - 1)),
Sheet:=CompSheet

End Sub
```

For example, the API function "SetDecisionVariables" identifies the ranges of cells in which decision variable values are stored. The user inputs the numbers of sources, DCs and customers along with a threshold for improvement between iterations as model parameters. After the user activates a "run" button displayed on a worksheet, a heuristically determined feasible solution to the nonconvex optimization problem is output into the right-hand side of the worksheet, prescribing order lot sizes for each DC as well as point-to-point flows, and total cost of transportation and cycle inventory. The total cost of this feasible solution serves as an upper bound against which a theoretical lower bound determined by the mathematical programming approximation is compared, and the relative gap is reported in percent.

Another UDF employing Bing maps API computed the road distance between nodes, which is multiplied by unit transportation cost parameters. Several adjustments were made to determine actual costs in the current plan employed by 2J for purposes of comparison to the plan prescribed by our model. The number of units sold in the season was 7,871 and the number purchased during the same period was 6,724 units. Inbound logistics costs were therefore multiplied by $1.17 \approx 7{,}871/6{,}724$, and holding and transaction costs were multiplied by $1.08 \approx \sqrt{7871/6724}$.

10.2 Design Principles Applied

As typical of the prescriptive stages of analytics, our system of visualization idioms was developed to communicate "discovered intelligence to the end audience" (Bendoly 2016, 2). The specific idioms employed were geographical maps, graphical plots of cycle inventory over time and a set of bar charts displaying inbound volumes from suppliers at each DC. To avoid cognitive overload, separate maps were created for inbound and outbound transportation flows, and the latter category further divided by large and small customers. This presentation of materials applies the Principles of Good Gestalt discussed in Chapter 2 of this volume. Examples of the idioms are given below. "Discovered intelligence" comprised heuristically determined solutions to the model as output by Open Solver, i.e. the order lot sizes, order frequencies and levels of product flows inbound from suppliers to distribution centers, and outbound from distribution centers to customers, for Freon. In a sense, the Gestalt of the system of idioms reflects the underlying Gestalt of the mathematical modeling, which integrates these supply chain management decisions within a single optimization model.

The end audience consists of the managers at 2J making decisions about transportation and inventory at both tactical and strategic levels. Specifically, the manager in the buyer/planner role is responsible for tactical-level purchasing, placing product orders and managing inventory to fulfill customer orders, along with managing supplier business allocation, order tracking, shipping and receiving, and all other factors associated with end-item inventory management. Relevant to this project, management is responsible for the strategic activities of allocation of work among the distribution centers and supplier selection. For these managers, the unit of analysis is the product family, which is an aggregation of two part numbers in our pilot project.

VBA output includes geographic characterization of the nodes representing suppliers, distribution centers and customers. Nodes have attribute data such as business name, address, geographic location and volume. There is also linkage data on the network, which tie suppliers to DCs, and DCs to customers through defined lanes. Decision variables indicate the lot sizes, frequencies and total volume level for product flows between suppliers and distribution centers, and from distribution centers to customers.

Once results are generated by the heuristic, we employed two complementary approaches to communicating the solution output: tables and visualization idioms. Presenting results in tables seems quite natural to the program developer since the underlying data has a tabular format, with identified nodes having multiple attributes at each level of the model. The primary advantage of presenting tabulated results is the precision with which information is communicated. The exact order quantities and timing can be read directly from the table. However, there are disadvantages to tables. Because there are 750 nodes in our example, the tabulated data without summaries and specific transformation is too large to be understood clearly and support defined decisions. Tabulated data can be summarized to improve recognition of relative amounts and identify potential choke points in the network. These summarized entries can then support drill-down capabilities to understand the detail. The design principle we deployed was to organize information flow from the direction of the DC for both supplier flow data and customer flow data. Table 10.1 below illustrates one example, which provides inbound flow amounts from each supplier, organized by DC. The data is the aggregated total volume for the season from each supplier.

Now consider the visual idioms we employed to convey the solution. The first is an inventory chart showing order lot sizing and frequency from two suppliers to a DC, Figure 10.2. From this view we can quite clearly understand the relative magnitudes of the two suppliers as well as the order timing and inventory impact of this plan. Figure 10.3 then displays the geographic data showing flows from sources to DCs. From this perspective we note the geographic dispersion of the supply plan, as well as the relative volume sourced from each depicted by the size of the icon. Particular supply routes can be emphasized by choice of colors as in Figure 10.4.

Gardner and Cooper (2003, 39) stated that a "well-constructed supply chain map with the right information, easily displayed and understood, should enhance the environmental scanning function of strategic planning." Visual displays can serve as a communication medium, knowledge management and decision support (Al-Kassab et al. 2014, 411). Market boundaries between DCs are made visible through the association of customers by color and number. In addition, clusters may represent opportunities for locating additional DCs, or conversely uncovering opportunities for consolidation.

Constructing such a map that specifically displays output from our optimization model was a primary goal of our pilot study. The integration of optimization with geographical mapping can be traced back to the pioneering work of Camm et al. (1997, 135) for Procter & Gamble. More recently, geographical mapping has been proposed by Bonanni (2010, 22) as a fundamental tool for designing

TABLE 10.1 Subset of Heuristically Determined Flows From Sources to 2J DCs

	Lexington	Louisville	Lima	Piketon	Corbin	
Supplier 1	135	596				1,180
Supplier 2		175				175
Supplier 3	350					350
Supplier 4				220		220
Supplier 5	413			126	381	920
Supplier 5			306			306
Supplier 6			98	264		4,720
Total	**898**	**771**	**404**	**610**	**381**	**7,871**
Order Quantity	109	101	73	90	71	

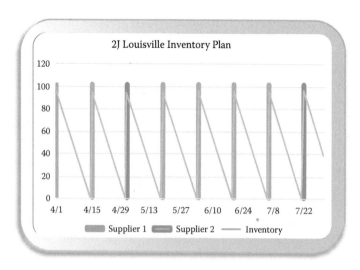

FIGURE 10.2 Lot Size, Frequency, and Relative Volume from Each Supplier

FIGURE 10.3 Inbound Flow Lanes Highlighted in Green

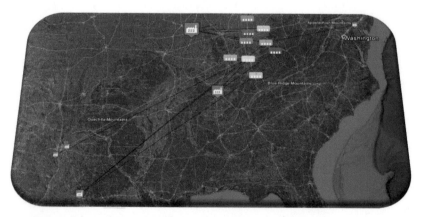

FIGURE 10.4 Inbound Lanes Highlighted in Red for Greater Visibility

sustainable supply chains, and an article in *Automotive Logistics* (Editorial Staff 2013, 12) discussed geographical mapping as a decision support tool for visualizing model output in an automotive supply chain. Consistent with the Law of Similarity cited in this volume, we show the within-group association of customers to distribution centers using common colors and numbering.

A low-cost and simple means of supply chain mapping is important for 2J since resources were limited for the pilot project both in terms of budget and information systems capabilities. Google Earth offers a simple and intuitive interface and is easy to program, so it was selected to serve as the display engine for this project. We use KML code, a variant of XML, for visual display (Open Geospatial Consortium 2016). To illustrate, consider the KML code below that generates a custom icon in Google Earth Pro:

```
1    <Folder><name>Styles</name>
2    <StyleMap id="DC_1">
3     <Pair><key>normal</key>
4           <styleUrl>#DC_1n</styleUrl>
5     </Pair>
6     <Pair><key>highlight</key>
7           <styleUrl>#DC_1_hover</styleUrl>
8     </Pair>
9    </StyleMap>
10
11   <Style id="DC_1n">
12    <IconStyle><scale>.75</scale>
13    <Icon><href>http://dl.dropboxusercontent.
      com/u/60426690/Icons/DC_1.png</href></Icon>
14    </IconStyle>
15    <LabelStyle><scale>0.0</scale></LabelStyle>
16    <BalloonStyle><text>$[description]</text>
      </BalloonStyle>
17   </Style>
18
19   <Style id="DC_1_hover">
20    <IconStyle><scale>1.0</scale>
21    <Icon><href>http://dl.dropboxusercontent.
      com/u/60426690/Icons/DC_1.png</href></Icon>
22    </IconStyle>
23    <BalloonStyle><text>$[description]</text>
      </BalloonStyle>
24   </Style>
25   </Folder>
26
27   <Folder><name>DistributionCenters</name>
28   <Placemark>
29    <name>DaytonWH</name>
```

```
30    <description><![CDATA[872 Valley St. Dayton, OH
45404]]></description>
31    <styleUrl>#DC_1</styleUrl>
32    <Point><coordinates>-84.1649340,39.7776600</
coordinates></Point>
33    </Placemark>
34    </Folder>
```

The first three blocks of code define the shape and behavior of icons with style parameters. Code can be compartmentalized in folders, as in line 1 of the code. Note the closing element in line 25. This allows blocks of code to be turned on or off in the Google Earth browser. The <Style> element defines how a feature is displayed in the Earth Pro browser. Styles are addressed by a user-defined id (line 11). <IconStyle> has elements that define and scale the icon. Icon files were created in Microsoft PowerPoint and saved as PNG files using the Windows snipping tool. Files were modified using the GNU Image Manipulation Program (GIMP), and saved in a publicly available folder. The <LabelStyle> element is scaled to 0.0 so that the icon name is normally not visible. The <BalloonStyle> element allows display of specific text. The code to change display of an icon when the cursor points to it starts at line 2, the <StyleMap> method.

A few examples of geographical maps are presented below to illustrate the results from this study. The map in Figure 10.5 shows inbound logistics. The suppliers are displayed in blue factory-shaped icons, and the distribution centers are displayed as various-colored icons with four white rectangular truck docks. We see from the map that no supplier is centrally located for this network, and that three of the suppliers in Texas are significantly distant.

The next map, Figure 10.6, shows the distribution of large customers for this network, clustered around the Cincinnati area. Large customers overall represent

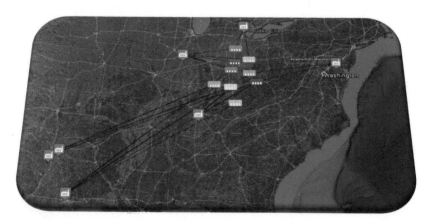

FIGURE 10.5 Inbound Logistics

FIGURE 10.6 Outbound Logistics—Cincinnati Large Customer

FIGURE 10.7 Outbound Logistics—Cincinnati Small Customers

about one half of total volume, and are eligible for provided delivery of product. We can contrast Figure 10.6 with Figure 10.7, small customers in the Cincinnati market. These customers average about two units of sales in season, and are more geographically dispersed than are the large customers. Note that in outbound maps, the hundreds of arcs between DCs and customers are not displayed, but rather implied by color-coding, in keeping with the Principles of Good Gestalt discussed in Chapter 2 of this volume.

To augment these geographic depictions, Figure 10.8 shows a simple dashboard displaying the inbound supply plan in current use by 2J, while Figure 10.9 shows a corresponding dashboard for the heuristically determined plan. Inbound unit logistics cost is graphed along the vertical axis to make distribution costs more apparent. Above each bar is shown the units of Freon shipped.

The objective of this display is to identify prescribed changes to the current plan, and then identify expensive logistics arrangements in the prescribed plan

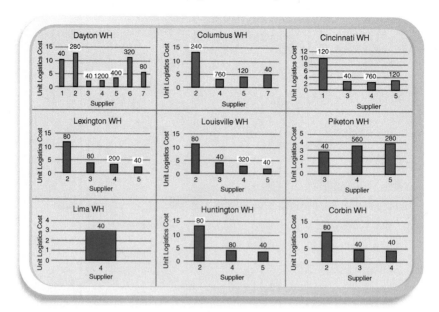

FIGURE 10.8 Current Inbound Logistics—Dashboard

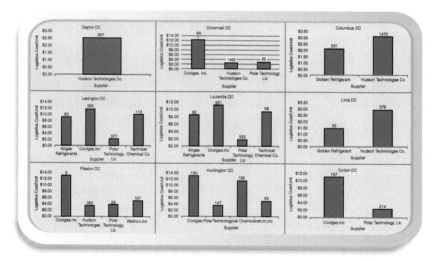

FIGURE 10.9 Model-Prescribed Inbound Logistics—Dashboard

with a view toward post-heuristic modifications. In other words, this display allows the user to perform a type of visual sensitivity analysis by identifying opportunities to modify the supply plan to reduce inbound logistics costs. Note that several DCs are assigned to costly suppliers. These adjustments can then be reviewed, and the optimization can be rerun with the modified supply plan with results

TABLE 10.2 Post-heuristic Improvement

	Plan 1	Plan 2	Actual (adjusted)
Holding Cost	4,972	4,272	4,274
Transaction Cost	4,972	4,972	6,428
Inbound Logistics	33,963	19,432	37,966
Outbound Logistics	13,879	13,879	15,031
Total	**57,786**	**43,255**	**63,699**

in Table 10.2. Plan 1 indicates the supply plan prescribed by the heuristic, while Plan 2 is revised to eliminate the expensive lanes, resulting in $14,531 in incremental savings.

10.3 Lessons for Future Development

In the first iteration of our proposed study, we used the General Algebraic Modeling System (GAMS) (GAMS Development Corporation) calling the CPLEX Solver to solve the optimization model. Although GAMS is a versatile high-level language that allows input from and output to an Excel workbook, use of this licensed product required a step outside of the worksheet environment. From conversations with the supply chain manager at 2J, it became clear that a completely workbook-based system would be more acceptable to management. Thus we adopted the Open Solver Excel add-in. From these conversations it also emerged that a notable benefit of geographical mapping is a better understanding of distribution patterns and the potential for this type of analysis to be used and hence contribute value to the supply chain. Currently, small customers pick up product rather than have it delivered, as is the case with larger customers. On viewing the map of customer locations, the Supply Chain Manager realized that there is the potential to deliver product to all customers of a DC in an efficient manner. The idea is to sell to the small customers early in the season, then deliver to all small customers early in the season on an optimized distribution pattern.

This approach is more efficient than having each customer drive to the DC individually and has the beneficial strategic effect of securing the sale early in the selling season, rather than hoping customers will arrive later in the season. Table 10.3 describes this plan in more detail. DCs are identified by a Division index. Total volume to all small customers of the DC is in column 2, followed by the number of small customers, which indicates the number of stops required. The model cost estimates column indicates the total logistics costs incurred by customers. Delivery on defined routes has the potential to greatly reduce travel distances, and costs. Therefore, the actual delivery cost is likely to be lower than in the current model. The challenge in terms of supply chain governance is that 2J Supply is not currently incurring any cost for delivering to these customers. Management will have to determine whether the strategic value of this new service is worth the incremental cost, and whether there is any potential for cost sharing with the customers. However, equipped with the tool piloted and described here, they are much better positioned to meaningfully consider their options.

The role of maps in spurring process improvement at 2J underscores Bendoly's (2016, 9) assertion that "putting visual renderings and interfaces for visual exploration into the hands of supply chain managers, for example, changes their behavior." It is also consistent with the experience of Camm et al. (1997), who noted that "often insights provided by the spatial visualization [of maps] led to new and better options" for product strategy at Procter & Gamble. It is also instructive to consider our visualization idioms as presented in Table 10.4 according to the framework of Pierce's Semiotics, as adapted by Bendoly (2016) and applied in Chapter 3 in this volume. A numeral in parentheses indicates the level in the framework, 1, 2, or 3, that best corresponds to each item. In this adapted framework, our idioms belong to schemas 2-2-2, 1-2-2 and 2-2-2, respectively. These schemas indicate a moderate "richness" of data visualization that can be presented to the end audience by way of our chosen idioms without causing information overload.

Broadly speaking, analytical results are often difficult to communicate to practicing managers without visual tools, particularly where there are a large number of data points involved as was the case with this project. The principles of design for data visualization help the researcher choose the appropriate set of idioms. In this case, as it features supply chain optimization, geographical maps, inventory

TABLE 10.3 Adding Delivery Service to Small Customers

Distribution Center	Small Customer Volume	Number of Stops	Model Cost Estimate
Division 1	590	129	$790.77
Division 3	757	141	$1,104.38
Division 5	354	83	$873.97
Division 7	450	58	$1,075.71
Division 9	589	104	$937.47
Division 11	355	66	$607.55
Division 13	419	54	$897.55
Division 15	329	43	$955.45
Division 17	129	19	$473.68
Total	**3,972**	**697**	**$7,716.53**

TABLE 10.4 Visualization Idioms in Adapted Semiotic Framework

Intended Message	Properties Connected	Depiction as Idiom
Order timing and allocation from each DC to prescribed suppliers (2)	Lot size, timing, and inventory level (2)	Inventory chart (2)
Customer allocation pattern to each DC (1)	Physical distribution of customers, assignment to DCs (2)	Geographical maps with color/number assignments (2)
Exploration of alternative supply plans (2)	Lane cost, volume, location over (2)	Dashboard (2)

charts and dashboards provide solutions in an intuitively appealing way even for managers lacking an understanding of the underlying mathematics. Managers can use these tools for both design and execution of decisions. Good Gestalt, such as color-coding to allow instantaneous mental sorting of the output showing customer to DC assignments, enhance the value of heuristic solutions for the firm. The use of open source and commonly available tools lowers the barriers to entry for this work. By sticking with commonly available software products, application, maintenance and revision become more feasible in the small business context.

References

Al-Kassab, Jasser, Zied M. Ouertani, Giovanni Schiuma, and Andy Neely. 2014. "Information Visualization to Support Management Decisions." *International Journal of Information Technology & Decision Making* 13 (2):407–428. doi: 10.1142/S0219622014500497.

Bendoly, Elliot. 2013. *Excel Basics to Blackbelt.* New York, NY: Cambridge University Press.

Bendoly, Elliot. 2016. "Fit, Bias, and Enacted Sensemaking in Data Visualization: Frameworks for Continuous Development in Operations and Supply Chain Management Analytics." *Journal of Business Logistics* 37 (1):1–12. doi: 10.1111/jbl.12113.

Bonanni, Leo. 2010. "Sourcemap: Eco-design, Sustainable Supply Chains, and Radical Transparency." *XRDS: Crossroads, The ACM Magazine for Students* 17 (4):22–26.

Camm, Jeffrey D., Thomas E. Chorman, Franz A. Dill, James R. Evans, Dennis J. Sweeney, and Glenn W. Wegryn. 1997. "Blending OR/MS, Judgment, and GIS: Restructuring P&G's Supply Chain." *Interfaces* 27 (1):128–142.

Editorial Staff. 2013. "Three OEMs Join Forces to Map Supply Chain." *Automotive Logistics*, 12–12.

Gardner, John T., and Martha C. Cooper. 2003. "Strategic Supply Chain Mapping Approaches." *Journal of Business Logistics* 24 (2):37–64.

General Algebraic Modeling System (GAMS) Release 24.2.1, Washington, DC, USA, 2013.

Mason, Andrew. 2012. "OpenSolver – An Open Source Add-in to Solve Linear and Integer Progammes in Excel." Operations Research Proceedings 2011, Heidelberg.

Mason, Andrew. 2016. "OpenSolver API Reference." http://opensolver.org/opensolver-api-reference/ [accessed April 3, 2016].

Open Geospatial Consortium. 2016. "KML." Open Geospatial Consortium [accessed February 9, 2016].

11

THE LONG WAY TO INTUITIVE VISUAL ANALYSIS OF AIR TRAFFIC CONTROL DATA

Paul Rosenthal, Linda Pfeiffer,
Nicholas Hugo Müller and Georg Valtin

The work of air traffic controllers is largely conducted in one of two arenas: the tower from which air traffic at and around an airport is supervised and controlled, and the area control center from which all other sectors of the relevant air space are controlled. In these area control centers, many sectors are managed by a dyad of air traffic controllers. The need for two controllers mainly originates from redundancy and work-division reasons. Both have access to all task relevant information, such as radar data, weather reports, and flight schedules (see Figure 11.1). A comprehensive discussion of the interrelations between air traffic controllers, their tasks, and the available interfaces was published by Smolensky and Stein (1998).

The main challenges of visual analytics in the field of air traffic control are:

- the highly specialized user group of air traffic controllers, which can hardly be modeled on basis of other user experiments;
- the high economic importance of the use case, making already small improvements significant due to massive economic savings;
- the extensive safety requirements, reducing innovation speed to a minimum due to long-lasting test and certification procedures.

This is also why it seems that the systems, currently in productive use, are designed quite conservatively and why they still often leverage old radar screen designs. In contrast, the air traffic itself has changed dramatically over the last few decades, along with its economic impact (see Figure 11.2).

Air traffic controllers have to handle much more traffic than they had to handle thirty years ago. In addition, airlines nowadays expect the air traffic controllers to

FIGURE 11.1 Work Position of Two Air Traffic Controllers; Area Control Center in Langen, Germany

Source: Image courtesy of DFS Deutsche Flugsicherung GmbH

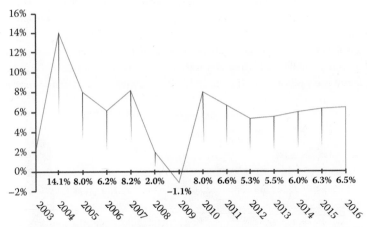

FIGURE 11.2 Annual Growth Rate of Passenger Kilometers Performed in Air Traffic Since 2003

facilitate the shortest possible routes for the aircraft to save fuel and time. All these conditions mandate much higher levels of efficiency among air traffic controllers; as well as much more effective decision-making capabilities. This can only be achieved if the human–machine interfaces are designed with a careful and contemporary view of an air traffic controller's tasks.

11.1   Appreciating the Audience and Context

To be sure, research and the practical consideration of data visualizations in air traffic control settings are not novel. In fact, this area has a long tradition due to the high information load the air traffic controllers have long faced in combination with the relevance of proper judgement driven by such information. With the increase in air traffic numbers throughout the last few decades, the information load each air traffic controller has to handle has significantly increased. Consequently, supporting technologies have had to be regularly reevaluated, even if updates have not been universal, making research in this field an ongoing effort. An overview of current developments and directions in this field was recently presented by Pfeiffer et al. (2015a). One noticeable trend in this field is the significant influence of available technology on research and applied methods. For example, once touch-enabled or stereoscopic displays were deemed reliable enough for productive use, it was proposed that they were used in order to make air traffic control more efficient (Stammers and Bird 1980; Lange et al. 2006; see for illustrative example Figure 11.3).

Similar discussions emerged from the invention of interactive e-ink displays, effectively allowing, in theory, the replacement of the paper flight strips (Doble and Hansman 2002; Hurter et al. 2012; Letondal et al. 2013; see Figures 11.4 and 11.5) or the introduction of head-mounted displays, enabling the usage of virtual- and augmented-reality methods in air traffic control (Reisman and Brown 2006).

Regardless of advances such as these, not all theoretical benefits anticipated in initial designs actually make their way into reality. This "realization-gap" is not only true for the use case of air traffic control, but for many other operator-dependent

FIGURE 11.3 Concept Study of the Air Traffic Controllers' Work Console of the Future

Source: Image courtesy of DFS Deutsche Flugsicherung GmbH

FIGURE 11.4 Electronic Flight Strip Display with Touch Input; Area Control Center in Bremen, Germany

Source: Image courtesy of DFS Deutsche Flugsicherung GmbH

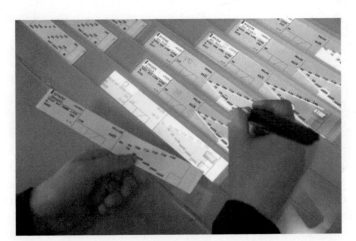

FIGURE 11.5 Strip'TIC: Mixing Electronic Flight Strips with Augmented Paper Tangibles

Source: Image courtesy of the Interactive Computing Laboratory at Ecole Nationale de l'Aviation Civile

high-risk business fields. Most of the application-related studies manage only to show marginal benefits in user performance with the application of new technologies. The difficulty is largely attributed not to a single failing technology, although clearly there are instances in which a lack of fit between process needs and technology support exist (see Chapter 3). More often in these settings, performance shortfalls can be attributed to a mismatch between newly adopted and legacy technologies and processes.

Furthermore, it is also evident that the restriction of a visualization and interaction design to work with a specific technology artifact highly constrained system outcomes. In contrast, the ideal visual analysis design process should always include a consequent abstract analysis of the data, the people, the environment, and the tasks. The analysis should be followed by a prototyping phase, which utilizes steady user input to move from abstract mockups to usable prototypes, eventually also defining hardware requirements. This yields an important take-away message:

> Don't let hardware dictate your visual analysis design.
> The best solution can only be generated if hardware follows productive design.

A common approach in today's visual analysis projects is to gather a reasonable set of possible designs, evaluate them with respect to the particular use case and environment, and to adapt the designs to fit the specific needs. Although there are quite a few very enlightening books (Ware 2008; Munzner 2014; Ward et al. 2015) which present a broad overview, it can be fairly hard to keep track of the different directions suggested. Furthermore, it can be quite hard to judge the applicability of a presented approach just from a publication. Indeed, to our knowledge, this book provides the first integrated resource linking comprehensive scientific arguments to specific case examples of successful application.

11.2 Design Principles Applied

As noted before, the variety of seemingly reasonable approaches to visualization, and human–computer interaction in general, is enormous. Hence, the main challenges for visual analytics researchers interested in tackling real world problems include: (a) managing the resource requirements for respective projects, and (b) adapting appropriate state of the art technology solutions to the needs of the particular use case. These challenges are far from straightforward. Available funding opportunities, for example, often don't match the requirements of real world development. In this respect, one must approach translational projects such as these with an eye on ongoing and perhaps diverse (public and private) funding opportunities.

With respect to the illustrated project, the use case and contact was already collected by the first author nearly five years before the project initiation, during a visit at an area control center. Here, already some challenges and possible directions for improvement, in terms of the visual analysis of air traffic data, arose in some informal discussions. Several years later, the German Federal Ministry of Education and Research issued a call for projects in the area of human–machine interfaces with special focus on emotional and cognitive considerations. Many translational research problems touch multiple organizational functions in their outcomes and hence benefit from a variety of disciplinary expertise. Accordingly, this call was discussed by a well-established interdisciplinary group of researchers. The discussion was carried out in an all-open fashion, meaning it was clear that the involvement of principle investigators might vary over the life of the project; or that new researchers might in fact ultimately be needed to tackle specific areas of the project. Such a model facilitates the development of intelligent and flexible designs for fit, in contrast to hierarchically steered process. The researchers in this case consisted of computer scientists, electrical engineers, and cognitive scientists.

Lastly, experience has shown that associated interdisciplinary discussions require openness as well as respect. They can also be very difficult to moderate, without an a priori understanding of shared goals and views on the systematic nature of the problem; as well as a focal point for design considerations. In this case the focal point that emerged from the discussions was the need to recognize the emotional state of two persons, working on a collaborative task, and design the user interface accordingly.

Two air traffic controllers are together responsible for one air space sector. They are required to process a high volume data in a very safety-sensitive environment, and rely on a human–computer interface to do so. It was immediately clear that such a use case was not possible to investigate without the support of actual users, i.e. DFS, the German air navigation service provider. A visit by three researchers out of the group of project applicants provided multiple benefits. To begin with, this provided a much more accurate view of the use case, as well as an early opportunity to soundboard our project ideas with the users. In addition, we were able to present our project concept to higher-level decision makers in detail, define requirements and limitations from both sides, define key players and their tasks, and finally convince them to join in. This also paved the way to a reliable connection for writing a common proposal and conducting the common research project.

In a partnered development relationship such as this, prior to the start of development work it is absolutely critical to consider issues such as intellectual property, nondisclosure, and data security; factors which are typically already regulated in a consortium agreement but not necessarily on the forefront of the minds of researchers/designers. All sides should carefully review their work packages, typical other work flows, common practices, as well as future plans, and openly communicate these among the project partners to check for possible implications or related requirements. Potential fields of action may certainly include publication regulations, reproducibility issues, different interpretation of work-package descriptions, or, especially important in the field of visual analytics, limitations regarding user studies.

Cultures and unwritten laws can differ widely among project partners. A joint project has the greatest likelihood of shared returns when all sides communicate their expectations, as well as any regulations regarding the project-related work, in advance and agree to a common project path.

In our project with the German air navigation service provider, some rules were very clear from the beginning. The work place of the air traffic controllers is located in a highly secured environment, with special protection against hardware disruptions, software or data manipulations, and interception of communication channels. Furthermore, the profession is highly dependent on the personal perceptual and cognitive skills of the individual air traffic controllers. Protecting them from overt or intrusive performance measurement is viewed as critical (and something that employee representatives reinforce). However, in developing an understanding of the context, our team recognized that scrutinizing the alternate workflows, solution strategies, interaction methods, and respective cognitive load of the controllers would be essential as well. These investigations could only be carried out with direct involvement of the employee representatives, strict anonymization, and acceptance of deep cuts in the collection of possible tools and approaches for studying the users. The tests with real users and additional measuring equipment were so far carried out at a reproduction of a work position in the research and development department of DFS, see Figure 11.6.

The proposed designs in air traffic control are currently being evaluated in an additional user study. Our first studies are concentrating on the efficiency of different visual encodings of two-dimensional air spaces; see Figure 11.7 (a). In the test scenario, users are confronted with a steady snapshot of a sector in one of our possible visual encodings and requested to memorize the situation. After a short period of time, the users are confronted with an empty sector, see Figure 11.7 (b), and requested to reconstruct the traffic that was presented before. We further used this case to initiate an investigation of the mental processes involved in organizing

FIGURE 11.6 Staging and Measurement at the Research and Development Department of DFS

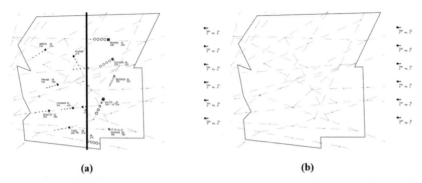

(a)   (b)

FIGURE 11.7 Visual Stimuli Used for Studying Air Space Encodings: (a) Two-dimensional Visualization of One Air Space Sector with a Side-by-side Comparison of Two Different Visual Encodings for Aircraft, Their Height, and Speed; (b) Empty Sector with Interactive Aircraft Symbols, which Can Be Used to Reproduce the Previous Situation

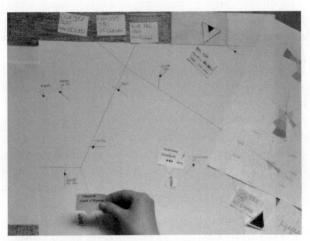

FIGURE 11.8 A Paper Prototype, Produced in the Design of the New Air Traffic Control Interface

air traffic with several on-site user studies and surveys (Pfeiffer et al. 2015c). Within, we discuss the various scenarios where it might be necessary for a controller to mentally visualize the airspace, what known stressors (e.g. unexpected events in the airspace) might occur, and how consequential physiological factors like arousal influence the psychological performance.

Finally, we focused on the combination of these factors and in what way they might be gathered and computed to analyze the workload of an air traffic controller, leading to a preliminary model regarding the mental state (Pfeiffer et al. 2015b). Many of these discussions rely on fast and flexible generation of mockups and prototypes, ideally on-site. Here, paper prototyping, see Figure 11.8, has again and again shown to provide the best properties.

11.3 Lessons for Future Development

From the air traffic controllers' perspective, most of our industry contacts viewed the work as a positive step forward. Many were impressed with how fundamental the air traffic control work flow was as a guiding principle throughout the project; Our development process in fact led them to question practices with long traditions. Collectively the project also yielded associated benefits to measurement practice in this setting. For example, standardized tests regarding mental capabilities (e.g. FAIR-2) are widely used and considered to be very robust. However, when using such tests to assess the capabilities of air traffic controllers, the established tests were simply just not robust enough. This is because the main idea of focus and attention tests is to put subjects into a situation where there is not enough time to complete all the tasks before the next one comes up.

As it turns out, air traffic controllers can in fact manage to complete these tasks within the given time frame—although these tasks were specifically designed not to be able to be finished. Hence our investigated user group belongs to the top 5 percent of subjects ever studied with this approach. Which makes such assessments in this context ultimately less informative in visual design processes. If augmenting focus and attention through visual design is a key objective, in this setting designers will have to change the standard tests or look for alternatives. Without our findings, who knows how much wasted effort might be allocated in future development processes.

Albeit an outstanding example of the byproducts of visual design processes, this was certainly not the first time that we encountered how important it is to validate all assumptions about the use case in practice. This especially means to not only review domain-specific literature and ask domain experts how the users most likely act, but actually to ask the active users and observe them. In doing so, for example, we showed that for most air traffic controllers operating in this context, currently the main functional planning devices were not highly sophisticated digital interfaces but rather the flight strips. The radar screen is mainly used as a system for checking if the respective aircraft are really acting as advised and as a backup system for the mental representation of the controller.

Acknowledgements

This work was partially supported by the Germany Federal Ministry of Education and Research in the project "StayCentered—Methodenbasis eines Assistenzsystems für Centerlotsen (MACeLot)." Furthermore, we thank the German air navigation service provider DFS Deutsche Flugsicherung GmbH for their support.

References

Doble, N.A., R.J. Hansman. 2002. Preliminary Design and Evaluation of Portable Electronic Flight Progress Strips, *Proceedings of the Digital Avionics Systems Conference*, 7C2-1–7C2-8.

Hurter, C., R. Lesbordes, C. Letondal, J. Vinot, S. Conversy, 2012. Strip'TIC: Exploring Augmented Paper Strip for Air Traffic Controllers, *Proceedings of the International Working Conference on Advanced Visual Interfaces*, 225–232.

Lange, M., T. Dang, M. Cooper. 2006. Interactive Resolution of Conflicts in a 3D Stereo-scopic Environment for Air Traffic Control, *Proceedings of the International Conference on Research, Innovation, and Vision for the Future*, 32–39.

Letondal, C., C. Hurter, R. Lesbordes, J. Vinot, S. Conversy. 2013. Flights in My Hands: Coherence Concerns in Designing Strip'TIC; A Tangible Space for Air Traffic Controllers, *Proceedings of the SIGCHI Conference on Human Factors in Computing Systems*, 2175–2184.

Munzner, T. 2014. *Visualization Analysis and Design*. AK Peters/CRC Press.

Pfeiffer, L., N.H. Müller, P. Rosenthal. 2015a. A Survey of Visual and Interactive Methods for Air Traffic Control Data, *Proceedings of the International Conference on Information Visualisation*, 574–577.

Pfeiffer, L., N.H. Müller, G. Valtin, M. Truschzinski, P. Protzel, P. Ohler, P. Rosenthal. 2015b. Emotionsmodell für zukünftige Mensch-Technik-Schnittstellen zur Unterstützung von Centerlotsen, *Proceedings der 57. Fachausschusssitzung Anthropotechnik der DGLR*, 219–232.

Pfeiffer, L., G. Valtin, N.H. Müller, P. Rosenthal. 2015c. Aircraft in Your Head: How Air Traffic Controller Mentally Organize Air Traffic, *Proceedings of HUSO, the International Conference on Human and Social Analytics*, 19–24.

Reisman, R., D. Brown. 2006. Design of Augmented Reality Tools for Air Traffic Control Towers, *Proceedings of the Aviation Technology, Integration and Operations Conference*.

Smolensky, M., E. Stein. 1998. *Human Factors in Air Traffic Control*. Academic Press.

Stammers, R.B., J.M. Bird. 1980. Controller Evaluation of a Touch Input Air Traffic Data System: An "Indelicate" Experiment, *Human Factors*, 22(5): 581–589.

Ward, M.O., G. Grinstein, D. Keim. 2015. *Interactive Data Visualization: Foundations, Techniques, and Applications, Second Edition*. AK Peters/CRC Press.

Ware, C. 2008. *Visual Thinking: For Design*. Morgan Kaufmann.

12

DATA VISUALIZATION IN HISTORY

David J. Staley

The historian who wishes to visualize data faces a number of challenges. In the first place, most historians would deny that they work with "data." As Christof Schoech has written,

> Most of my colleagues in literary and cultural studies would not necessarily speak of their objects of study as "data." If you ask them what it is they are studying, they would rather speak of books, paintings and movies; of drama and crime fiction, of still lives and action painting; of German expressionist movies and romantic comedy. They would mention Denis Diderot or Toni Morrison, Chardin or Jackson Pollock, Fritz Lang or Diane Keaton. Maybe they would talk about what they are studying as texts, images, and sounds. But rarely would they consider their objects of study to be "data."
>
> *(Schoech 2013)*

The same is true of historians, who would not describe the materials they work with as data, but as evidence or records or documents or primary sources. "Data" has connotations of numbers and statistics and sounds a little too much like social science for the comfort of many historians. Indeed, there was once a thriving "cliometrics" movement in history in the 1970s and 1980s, whose more aggressive practitioners contended that only those data from the past that were measurable and quantifiable, subject to statistical analysis, were legitimate sources of historical inquiry. While there remains a subfield of quantitative history, a "quantitative turn" never fully materialized in history. As a result, many historians continue to equate "data" with quantities and not necessarily with their work.

Ironically, social science history faded just as computers became widely available, just as new kinds of social science history became feasible. No longer is there any need for white-coated attendants at huge mainframes and expensive proprietary software. Rather than reducing people to rows and columns, searchable databases now permit researchers to maintain the identities of individuals in those databases and to represent entire populations rather than samples. Moreover, the record can now include things social science history could only imagine before the web: completely indexed newspapers, with the original readable on the screen; completely searchable letters and diaries by the thousands; interactive maps with all property holders identified and linked to other records. Visualization of patterns in the data, moreover, far outstrip the possibilities of numerical calculation alone. Manipulable histograms, maps, and time lines promise a social history that is simultaneously sophisticated and accessible. We have what earlier generations of social science historians dreamed of: a fast and widely accessible network linked to cheap and powerful computers running common software with well-established standards for the handling of numbers, texts, and images. New possibilities of collaboration and cumulative research beckon. Perhaps the time is right to reclaim a worthy vision of a disciplined and explicit social scientific history that we abandoned too soon.

(Ayers 1999)

For purposes of this chapter, then, if we are going to use the term "data" in history we mean the kinds of documents that historians work with: that "data" is a synonym for records, documents, primary sources and the like.

12.1 Appreciating the Audience and Context

Apart from conceptual and terminological difficulties, another challenge historians wrestle with when seeking to visualize our data is that our data are very often "incomplete." In some cases, as with historians working with Parliamentary or Congressional records, where speeches are recorded, we might assume a "complete" account of the debates of the legislature. But historians also understand that our records, as they are being created, are but a partial record of events, and cannot capture all of the happenings of the past:

> Historians ... do not possess infinite data, indeed, they are lucky to possess data at all. They are in no position to generate data of their own, but must take whatever people in the past, for their own purposes, deemed appropriate to collect and record, winnowed by the inevitable losses of documentation wrought by the passage of time ... Rather than asking "What are the most relevant questions that I should ask about a particular process?", historians must say, "Here are my data, what questions can I answer with them?"
>
> *(Thornton 1990)*

Further, the records historians consult are frequently scattered among many locations, and because they are so scattered, we cannot assume that the same metadata protocols have been followed, and so the interoperability of these data cannot be assumed. This is assuming, of course, that those data have been digitized at all, let alone digitized along the same standard. Most of the data historians work with are not born digital (they exist as physical documents) and so the range of data that we can visualize is constrained by the amount of such records that archivists and librarians (and commercial firms like ProQuest) have digitized (Borgman 2015).

That number remains relatively small.

The above illustrates the degree to which historians rely on others to provide them with data. While the historian most certainly gathers and marshals sources, these are curated by others. We work closely with archivists, who are the ones who would be responsible for digitizing the data. In contrast to social scientists, for example, historians are typically neither the creator nor the curator of their data. There are exceptions to this pattern: the Valley of the Shadow project is an example of historians taking the lead to digitize documents, with historians playing the role of curator. Indeed, many of the early digitalization projects of the early 2000s were led by historians or centers associated with history departments. More typical, however, are the Library of Congress's American Memory Project and the digitalization efforts of the National Archives. Early English Books Online (EEBO) has proven to be an important tool for historians of early modern Europe and colonial America. Each of these digitalization projects have been driven by archives and archivists.

A social scientist typically creates their own data by conducting a survey, designing a questionnaire or engaging in some sort of experiment. Historians rarely have the opportunity to "create data" in this fashion. There are notable exceptions: historians who engage in oral history—in structured interviews with participants of historical event—do indeed have the opportunity to create their own data. I've a colleague who is studying the history of the AIDS crisis in San Francisco who is collecting pamphlets, mimeographed newsletters and other artifacts of the scene from the 1980s, a task that usually falls to the archivist. But these are exceptions to the general rule that historians work in archival collections, with data curated by others.

If historians deny that they work with data, then "visualization" proves even more problematic (Staley 2013). Historians define their professional practice largely through the presentation of words. Scholarly performance in history is determined by writing an article, publishing a monograph or reading a paper aloud at a conference. Visual performances are outside the pale of our professional practice, and indeed historians tend to distrust visual performances as being little more than illustrative of arguments made and analysis undertaken in written form. The historian John Lukacs has written that:

> Technology has made pictorial presentations of this or that history more and more possible ... Pictorial representations of scenes or episodes or persons

may give the impression of something direct, three-dimensional, accurate, real: but in reality their production is very complicated, resulting in images and people seeming "true" but often not true enough.

(Lukacs 2011)

Lukacs expresses an extreme view, perhaps, but his disposition toward the visual is very much in line with the attitudes of most historians. The historian who wishes to visualize his data has few peer-reviewed publication options. We have very few cultural and intuitional practices that sustain the visual and visualization. Museums exhibitions and other forms of visual display are largely outside the practice of professional historians; it would be difficult for a professor employed by a Research 1 history department to have an exhibition, a film or other such visualization be considered a tenurable publication. Our journal articles and printed books leave little room for visualizations. Indeed, we maintain that the prose exposition is the main carrier of the meaning, the vehicle for the argument. Any visualizations we might include plays a supporting, secondary role to the written argument (for a notable exception see Ferster 2013).

With these challenges in mind, there are nevertheless historians who are engaged in pathbreaking work on data visualization.

12.2 Design Principles Applied

Digital Mapping

The most common form of data visualization would be digital mapping. While historians have largely shied away from visualization and the analysis visualization affords, this is not as true of maps. Maps have long had a place in our professional practices, but largely as illustrative artifacts created after the analysis has been completed, not as the carrier of the analysis.

Projects undertaken by the Spatial History Project at Stanford are noteworthy in the way that they take historical data and, by spatializing it, allow us to see hitherto unseen patterns. "Mapping the Law: The Evolution of Slaughterhouse Space, 1852–1870" maps out city and state laws that regulated the location of slaughterhouses within the city of San Francisco (for examples see: http://web.stanford.edu/group/spatialhistory/cgi-bin/site/index.php, accessed September 13, 2015).

Early zoning efforts relied on a concept of "negative space" to protect certain downtown neighborhoods from slaughterhouses and other nuisances. Later regulations evolved to establish finite slaughterhouse zones in an effort to effect certain environmental and spatial relationships for slaughterhouses within the city limits, far from downtown.

(Spatial History Project, http://web.stanford.edu/group/spatialhistory/cgi-bin/site/viz.php?id=409&project_id=1047, accessed January 12, 2016)

Mapping these laws allows the historian to uncover shifting geographic patterns that a reading of the laws would not necessarily reveal.

As another example, "Mapping Mobility in the Budapest Ghetto" (http://web.stanford.edu/group/spatialhistory/cgi-bin/site/viz.php?id=411&project_id=1015, accessed December 15, 2015) visualizes the activities of Jews in that city, revealing temporal boundaries beyond the physical boundaries imposed by ghettoization. In 1944, Jews in Budapest would have been permitted to leave their homes during a brief three-hour window in the afternoon. The severe temporal restrictions meant that, although they were free to move about the city, those movements were restricted by the time constraints. Given that they would need to wait in lines for food and other essentials, the actual physical spaces they might move through would have been constricted. This digital map visualizes these hitherto unseen temporal boundaries around movement.

The same source illustrates "The Evolution of the SS Concentration Camp System, 1933–1945," a seemingly straightforward enough task: a mapping of the Nazis' concentration camp system. The creators of this map are seeking to understand the patterns of concentration camp formation, and through the visualization seek to answer the following questions: "How was the location of camps related to resources and territorial control? Why did some camps exist only briefly while others lasted for years? Why did so-called "subcamp" openings accelerate in late 1944, and what explains their clustering? How were subcamps related to main camps? Were Allied advances responsible for the apparent consolidation of camps?" Spatializing what had hitherto been non-spatialized data reveals visual patterns that raise new questions for historians.

I am drawn to the Hypercities project at UCLA because it expands the kinds of data we can visualize on a map (www.hypercities.com, accessed November 12, 2015). The authors of Hypercities contend that what they are doing is "thick mapping," which they define as "the process of collecting, aggregating, and visualizing ever more layers of geographic or place specific data" (Presner et al. 2014). Unlike a GIS map, the kinds of data that are being visualized are not polygons but actual images, text, video and other forms of data and media imposed right on the map. The Hypercities project uses the map as a way to organize the data in a database: the map becomes the interface with that database, but simultaneously serves as the organization and analytic means. Scale and layering are also interesting properties of Hypercities: the ability to zoom in on details within the city, and to zoom out to examine the whole. Each layer of the scale has its own kinds of information, its own insights to draw. That is, the kind of information accessed at the city-level scale is not the same as the information found at the neighborhood or city street level. Further, Hypercities layers time on the city. One can zoom in on an image that depicts the activities and actions at that location at a time in the past. Thus, time is itself a layer in this form of mapping.

"Visualizing Emancipation" (http://dsl.richmond.edu/emancipation/, accessed November 22, 2015) is a mapping project that visualizes the end of slavery in the

South. Mapping various pieces of evidence—such as policies enacted by the government, actions on the battlefield and acts by enslaved men and women—demonstrates that emancipation was a process that occurred slowly and at differential rates. The researchers conclude that emancipation began even before the first battles of the Civil War, and was an ongoing process even after the War's conclusion. Mapping these events, visualizing our documentary records, affords us the opportunity to see these historical issues in a new light.

Network Visualizations

Some historians are employing network visualizations to visualize documents collected in a database. "Mapping the Republic of Letters," a project based at Stanford University, maps the exchange of over 55,000 letters and other documents between 6,400 correspondents that made up the seventeenth and eighteenth-century "Republic of Letters." At a time where there were few universities or research institutes, Enlightenment philosophers exchanged knowledge through a kind of invisible college. Using the Electronic Enlightenment database, these researchers have visualized the structure of this network, its location in time and space, the extent of the network and the evolution of the system over time (http://republicofletters.stanford.edu/; http://web.stanford.edu/group/toolingup/rplviz/, accessed January 2, 2016).

Historians at Harvard are collaborating on the Visualizing Historical Networks project (www.fas.harvard.edu/~histecon/visualizing/, accessed December 3, 2015). "The Inner Life of Empires" by Emma Rothschild visualizes the network of connections among the Johnston family, an eighteenth-century Scottish family. Max Schich (www.schich.info/, accessed December 3, 2015) and his colleagues have used the Freebase.com, the General Artist Lexicon (AKL), and the Getty Union List of Artist Names (ULAN) databases to map the locations of the birth and deaths of hundreds of notable historical figures (http://science.sciencemag.org/content/345/6196/558.full, accessed December 3, 2015).

> The resulting network of locations provides a macroscopic perspective of cultural history, which helps us to retrace cultural narratives of Europe and North America using large-scale visualization and quantitative dynamical tools and to derive historical trends of cultural centers beyond the scope of specific events or narrow time intervals.
>
> *(www.cultsci.net/, accessed December 3, 2015)*

Data Analytics

Some historians have also developed an interest in using data analytics and text mining techniques on our historical records, with a concomitant need to visualize the results. In looking at large databases of texts, such as the trial transcripts

of the Old Bailey (http://criminalintent.org/wp-content/uploads/2011/09/
Data-Mining-with-Criminal-Intent-Final1.pdf, accessed November 12, 2015)
historians are exploring macro-level patterns in those data. This represents a
methodological change in orientation for historians, who typically work via a
"close reading" of their texts. Data analytics techniques applied to entire cor-
puses of historical data expand the scale of historical investigation (Guldi and
Armitage 2014).

Robert K. Nelson and Scott Nesbit at the University of Richmond, in their
project "Mining the Dispatch" (http://dsl.richmond.edu/dispatch/, accessed
January 2, 2016) have been text mining the Richmond Daily Dispatch during the
Civil War. In one case, they tracked the number of articles they defined as "poetry
and patriotism," which were articles that "called on southern men to defend their
homes, their wives, and their sacred honor."

The number of such articles skyrockets in the early stages of the War, then
declines as the War progresses, with an uptick during the last few weeks of the
conflict. Similarly, articles defined as "anti-northern diatribes"—which were
"vitriolic ... viciously condemned northern society"—follow a similar pattern.
Indeed, when these two are visualized together, their rise and fall aligns almost
perfectly.

> These two topics—one extolling the selfless, brave southern soldier, the
> other condemning the selfish, vicious northern soldier and citizen—are
> two sides of the same coin ... Taken together they provide a register of
> when and how southern nationalism was deployed in the pages of the Dis-
> patch. The peaks during the first half of 1861, the spring of 1862, and the
> spring of 1865 correspond to the beginning of the war, the beginning of
> conscription in April 1862, and the end of the war.
>
> *(http://dsl.richmond.edu/dispatch/Topics, accessed January 2, 2016)*

12.3   Lessons for Future Development

My own work involves visualizing secondary sources, specifically articles in scholarly
journals. Graduate students are asked to master "the literature of the field," and they
read scores of books in preparation for PhD examinations. I wondered if we could
use similar data analytics procedures to examine the scholarly literature of a field.

Academic journals provide a useful source for such an inquiry, as journals represent as complete a "system" as we have. Many of these journals have been digitized
such that not only can they be searched but we can also find patterns in them. In
the same way Franco Moretti looked at all publications, not just canonical works,
I am considering all articles, not just those identified as seminal in the field.

David Mimno has employed topic modeling as a way to uncover such histo-
riographic patterns (Mimno 2012). Mimno in particular looked at classics journals, noting that articles in classics tend to be on one of two types: archeological

or philological. Using MALLET, he was able to identify the contents of an article to identify it as largely philological or archeological in orientation, and to uncover changing patterns over time.

My first experiment was conducted on the journal *The Florida Historical Quarterly*. We used the Data for Research tool provided by JSTOR. Relying on the IF-TDF method, Data for Research identifies the top key terms in a given article. We identified the top 100 key terms over the entire 85-year run of the journal. We then determined the frequency of those key terms per year, revealing a visualization of the changing patterns of topic coverage in the journal. In looking at key terms, we discerned that *The Florida Historical Quarterly* has long published articles on Native Americans, Florida's colonial history and the Seminole Wars. Most of the terms were eighteenth and nineteenth century in their orientation: terms related to Florida's twentieth-century history (space, retirement, Disney, animation, NASA, Orlando) were not to be found among the top 100. Arraying these terms in a 2-D visualization showed that articles in the first 30 or so years of the journal concentrated on a dozen or so key terms, but that over time the extent of topical coverage in the journal broadened. This is depicted in Figure 12.1 (adapted from Staley et al. 2014).

Using this same technique, I examined the journal *The Public Historian*. In this instance, I clustered comparable key terms together, which produced meaningful visual patterns. Notably, terms referring to professionals such as "historian" and "archivist" decline over time. Terms such as "museum," "visitor," "heritage" and

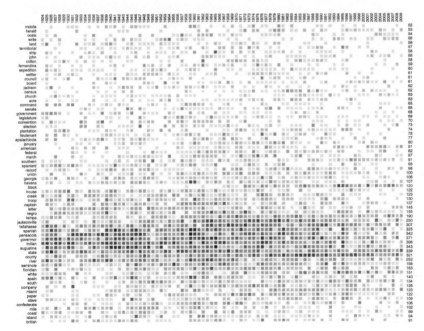

FIGURE 12.1 *The Florida Historical Quarterly*

"site" rise in importance over the life of the journal. My conclusion is that the topic focus of the journal had shifted by the early 2000s from a concern for the activities of professionals to a greater interest in visitor experience, and in popular representations of history.

Whenever I examine the intellectual history of an historical journal in this fashion, I look in particular for the key term "woman." Knowing something of the historiography of women's history and of a "gender turn" in historical scholarship, I was curious to determine the frequency of the key term. My expectation was that the term would only appear with any frequency after the 1970s, that is, after the subfield of women's history first established itself. Looking at the *American Historical Review*, for example, yielded a few references to "women" in the early days of the journal, but not until the mid-1980s could one see a sizeable number of articles with "women" as a key term. *The Florida Historical Quarterly*, on the other hand, did not witness such an increase in the key term until the mid-1990s. I wondered if other such journals exhibited this change at a similar rate. That is, did the gender turn in history occur simultaneously or at varying rates?

I looked at 20 history journals—none a specialized journal in women's history—as a way to gauge the rates at which the key term "woman" appeared. The journals that I visualized followed a similar pattern: few references to "women" until the mid-1980s, at which point there is a "take off" and the number of references skyrockets. Figure 12.2 provides this visualization.

But even within this general pattern, there are varying rates of change, as one journal had numerous references to women as early as the 1940s, and the afore-mentioned *The Florida Historical Quarterly* "lagging" into the 1990s. After designing this visualization, I asked my colleagues whether or not I had visualized "the gender turn in history."

I have turned some of my historical visualizations into physical objects. We have 3D printed a version of *The Florida Historical Quarterly*, with spiky ridges to represent the number of articles appearing in a given year. "Woman in History" is at the moment a visualization on paper, but I've plans to build this as a monumental installation, where a viewer would be able to walk through the data, the body

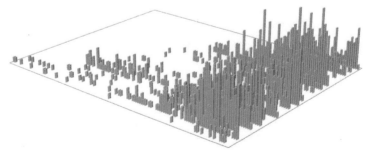

FIGURE 12.2 3D Digital Rendering of "Woman in History"

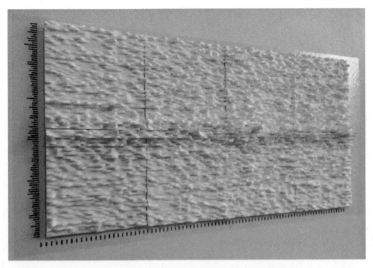

FIGURE 12.3 3D Printed Artifact Capturing "Woman in History"

moving through the space of the data as a way to experience the data. A rendering of this physical artifact is provided in Figure 12.3.

Data visualization offers the historian the chance to uncover hitherto unseen macro-level patterns in those data, yielding new insights and new understanding. As Nelson and Nesbit note, their projects:

> use digital tools and digital media to uncover and represent patterns that are not easy to find when we look at particular pieces of evidence in isolation and only become evident when we visualize a wealth of evidence in graphs, maps and models. Revealing patterns in text and across time and space, many of these visualizations are intriguing and surprising, offering us new insights.
> *(http://dsl.richmond.edu/civilwar/index.html, accessed December 12, 2015)*

In contrast to practitioners in other disciplines, historians approach data visualization (indeed all of our questions) not seeking prediction. Data visualization in many other fields is predicated on the assumption that the researcher can seize upon patterns in the data that yield better predictive models. In looking at the history of topical coverage in a journal, for example, I am not seeking some sort of predictive model of where the field might go in the future, but to understand something about how that field has evolved. Historians understand that complex adaptive systems are rarely so predictive, and most of the systems we are attempting to visualize are such complex systems. History has never really been about prediction, and our efforts to visualize are aimed at uncovering insight and meaning in those data.

References

Ayers, E.L. 1999. *The Pasts and Futures of Digital History*, www.vcdh.virginia.edu/PastsFutures. html [accessed December 7, 2015].

Borgman, C.L. 2015. *Big Data, Little Data, No Data: Scholarship in the Networked World*, Cambridge, MA: The MIT Press, 162.

Ferster, B. 2013. *Interactive Visualization: Insight Through Inquiry*, Cambridge: The MIT Press.

Guldi, J., D. Armitage. 2014. *The History Manifesto*, Cambridge, MA: Cambridge University Press, 88–116.

Lukacs, J. 2011. *The Future of History*, New Haven, CT: Yale University Press.

Mimno, D. 2012. Computational Historiography: Data Mining in a Century of Classics Journals, *Journal on Computing and Cultural Heritage* 5(1), Article 3.

Presner, T., D. Shepard, Y. Kawano. 2014. *Hypercities: Thick Mapping in the Digital Humanities*, Cambridge, MA: Harvard University Press.

Schoech, C. 2013. Big? Smart? Clean? Messy? Data in the Humanities, *Journal of Digital Humanities*, 2(3).

Staley, D.J. 2013. *Computers, Visualization, and History: How New Technology Will Transform Our Understanding of the Past*, 2nd Edition. New York, NY: Routledge.

Staley, D.J., S.A. French, B. Ferster. 2014. Visual Historiography: Visualizing "The Literature of a Field". *Journal of Digital Humanities*, 3(1).

Thornton, J. 1990. The Historian and the Precolonional African Economy. *African Economic History* 19, 45–54.

13

AN ENERGY INFORMATION SYSTEM TO CONSERVE ELECTRICITY IN CAMPUS BUILDINGS

Shaun Fontanella

Buildings use large amounts of energy to maintain their climates and provide building energy services. In 2014, buildings were responsible for 41 percent of total US energy use (EIA 2015b). In the US, the majority of energy is produced using fossil fuels. This production is responsible for emitting climate changing greenhouse gasses. Reducing a building's energy consumption will reduce its contribution to global climate change as well as other negative externalities associated with energy production like air pollution and water system degradation.

Unfortunately, energy conservation in buildings can be difficult for a host of reasons (Sovacool 2009). Some of these have to do with the modern nature of energy delivery and how energy is accounted for. Most energy is billed in unfamiliar units such as kilowatt hours and mBTUs. Consumers are not familiar with these units because they don't interact with them on a routine basis if at all. They understand gallons of gasoline because they buy milk, water and other goods in gallons but they do not understand kilowatt hours or mBTUs.

Time is another strike against energy conservation. Energy consumers are typically billed once every month instead of at the time of use like most other products and services. Consumers pay for food when they leave the grocery store, not a month later. However, energy is often paid for long after it is used. This temporal separation attenuates the connections between energy decisions and their outcomes.

Energy is delivered by complex networks of pipes and wires that hide the externalities associated with energy's production. Energy facilities are usually located down wind and out of sight of the consumers who use their services, especially affluent ones. These out of sight facilities emit pollutants far from the people who are responsible for their creation. The daily, local acts of chopping wood and shoveling coal into a furnace or stove, as well as the soot produced from those acts, are gone from American cities as is the connection between energy production and its consequences.

Finally, there is price. Compared to many countries, energy in the US is relatively inexpensive. Many consumers don't look closely at their energy bills. A kilowatt hour of electricity averages $.12 in the US compared to $.26 in Japan and $.41 in Denmark. This cheap energy is unlikely to change in the near future. As inexpensive energy is associated with strong economic growth, politicians and bureaucrats are reluctant to increase energy's price through taxes and regulation. The Californian electricity crisis in the early 2000s could have been significantly mitigated by removing the retail cap on electricity prices and sending the correct signals to the market but politicians found this option so politically unpopular they tolerated rolling brownouts and commercial price spikes rather than change the regulations (Yergin 2011).

In addition to the intrinsic nature of energy creating energy conservation difficulties, commercial buildings present distinct challenges of their own. Commercial buildings often have tenants who lease space from a building owner. The building owner does not pay the utilities and so has little incentive to invest in energy conservation for the whole building (Troy 2012). Commercial buildings often have common spaces where there is shared control of energy consuming services. These shared spaces create uncertain areas of control that dilute responsibility. For instance, a common hallway, lobby or bathroom may have its lights left on all night because nobody takes the initiative to turn them off or because of the perceived safety of well-lit areas. Either through apathy or courtesy, common areas in commercial buildings can pose a challenge to energy conservation.

Some commercial and institutional buildings, like those on university campuses, exhibit additional complications to energy conservation. In these buildings, there are multiple tenants but only one meter. The total energy bill has to be shared in some equitable manner so energy is paid for with a flat fee. The building is divided up between the tenants by percentage of occupied space and the bill is calculated by square foot. This flat fee model dilutes any financial incentive to conserve energy. Poor energy decisions by one tenant are masked by the total consumption of the building. Installing sub meters is expensive, has little payback for building owners and requires long term capital planning in institutions with many competing agendas.

On campuses, buildings have an inordinate amount of temporary occupants as students and faculty are often shifted around different campus buildings from semester to semester to take classes. These transitory occupants don't spend enough time in temporary buildings to know the norms of use. They default to leaving everything as it is instead of taking responsibility for energy consumption. Many campus classrooms have as much lighting as an entire house and those lights stay lit all night.

13.1   Appreciating the Audience and Context

Despite all of the previously described obstacles, there are examples of effective building energy conservation programs (Ehrhardt-Martinez, Donnelly, and Laitner 2010). Many of the successful programs work by providing building occupants with energy information through various information technology systems. These programs go by various names including advanced metering initiatives, building automation systems and energy information systems (EIS). While initial energy dashboards provided better access to energy data, most were designed for building managers. These managers are already familiar with building energy services. Because of this expert technical knowledge, many of these designs expressed information in units that were not comprehendible to the average building occupant.

This early focus on building managers was in part because EISs were expensive to install and operate. However, the standardization of web technologies, the spread of wireless networks and the explosion of cheap hardware have expanded the reach of building energy information through the installation of web-based energy dashboards (Capehart and Middelkoop 2011). These new systems are targeted at both building managers and occupants. They mix the traditional physical technical and engineering model with the behavioral model into a hybrid called socio-technical (Gulbinas, Jain, and Taylor 2014). Because they are designed to present data to a lay audience, it is important that they both address the problems of communicating energy information, and that they conform to best practices for data visualization and dashboard design (cf. Chapter 3, Bendoly 2016).

Of the programs documented in the literature, most were conducted in residential buildings or campus dormitories. In these spaces there is single user control of energy consuming services and appliances (Petersen et al. 2007). One user can see the outcomes of their own actions and compare their consumption to other single controlled spaces. There is a lack of research in commercial buildings and especially commercial buildings with shared occupancy and aggregated energy information (Lehrer and Vasudev 2011). Because they often have old and historic building stock, many colleges and universities are prime targets for aggregated energy building research.

13.2   Design Principles Applied

Using successful design principles found in the meta-analysis of residential programs compiled by Ehrhardt-Martinez et al., a socio-technical EIS was built in order to address the lack of research in commercial buildings with aggregated energy information. The EIS was installed in a building on the campus of Ohio State University. The EIS displays current and historical electricity consumption data from the test building on digital signage located at all entrances to the building. This information is also available online to any web connected computer or mobile device. The signage is installed in Mendenhall Lab, a four-story 124,000 square feet building typical for Ohio State University. It has a combination of classroom, lab, and office space. Mendenhall Lab was initially built in the early 1900s and was expanded twice but has undergone renovations that have brought its mechanical systems up to recent standards. Mendenhall Lab is one of the few buildings on the Ohio State University campus that has real time energy information available through a public interface.

The applied research analyzed by Ehrhardt-Martinez et al. describes several features of successful EISs. The more recent the data, the better. Real time data is the best. This type of data allows consumers to make connections between activities and consumption. Detailed use information was better than aggregated information. Detailed use information is an even more explicit way a consumer can connect an appliance or activity to energy consumption. The researchers also concluded that gadgets alone are not enough. The information provided by feedback devices has to be put in context in order to be understood. This could be historical context, comparison to other buildings, or compared to a standard or averaged consumption rate.

The proceeding principles were taken into account when designing the EIS. Figure 13.1 is a screenshot of the dashboard as it is displayed in the study building by default. The first metric of the row displays the current kW consumption of the building. An observer can click on a button to bring up a table with more information to put kWs into context. In the case of kilowatts, the EIS converts the current kW use into appliances that an observer might be familiar with (see Figure 13.2) including an iPhone charger, a traditional 60 watt incandescent lightbulb, and several classrooms in the building. The US housing equivalent is usually above 300 during weekdays.

On the right of the current kW consumption in Figure 13.1, the EIS translates this consumption into equivalent units that are used to produce that amount

FIGURE 13.1 Screenshot of Dashboard Displayed in Mendenhall Lab

Some Context for Kilowatts

Electric units of measurement can be hard to understand since we don't use them everyday. Here are some comparisons to make it clearer.

Item	Consumes	Current Building Use Equivalant
iPad Charger	12 Watts	22,500 iPad chargers
Incandescent Lightbulb	60 Watts	4,500 Lightbulbs
42 Inch LED TV	45 Watts	6,000 TVs
Hair Dryer	1500 Watts	180 Hair Dryers
Average U.S. Home	1250 Watts	216 Homes
Mendenhall 125 Classroom Lighting	900 Watts	300 Classrooms
Mendenhall 163 Lab Lighting	1675 Watts	161 Labs

close

FIGURE 13.2 Unit Conversions to Contextually Familiar References

of electricity or are the byproducts of the current building consumption. For instance, the current use is translated into the amount of coal that is burned per hour to deliver the current electricity load using calculation methods from the EIA (EIA 2015a). The EIS also translates into water consumed, pounds of carbon dioxide emitted, and cost in dollars per hour. Each one of these metrics has a table that converts that metric into the same consumption for common appliances or lighting uses.

In order to give the data context, one of the largest areas on the dashboard is dedicated to a trending graph. The graph is displayed in kilowatts because this is the unit electricity is measured in. This graph shows the electricity consumption of the building for the past nine hours. It also shows the previous year's data. This comparison lets the observer know whether the building is using less or more electricity than historical consumption. Even if the observer does not know how much energy is in a kW, it will be obvious how many the building is consuming compared to historical data. It should be noted that energy consumption in buildings can be drastically influenced by weather so the trend graph may at times be higher than historical use despite conservation efforts.

Another observation of the literature about successful programs is that the higher the rate of participation, the more successful an energy conservation program is. That is, defaulting to participation and making subjects opt out was found to be more successful than opt-in programs. Noting this, the EIS signage was placed at the entrances to the building so that every occupant entering the building could see the current electricity consumption. Everyone entering the building was by default opted into the study.

A sense of control is another important aspect of successful conservation efforts. Occupants must feel that they can act upon information delivered by the EIS. To address this principle, the EIS has a separate page that describes actions that building occupants can take to reduce the building total consumption. These include turning off lights, using thermostats instead of opening windows, and turning off unused equipment like computers and lab equipment. It also has contact information for maintenance personnel if occupants see broken equipment that may be affecting energy consumption.

The EIS design started with the electricity data and the principles discussed in the literature. It was also heavily influenced by the medium used to display it. Digital signage, and dashboard applications in general, are being transitioned to web standard technologies to display their information (Capehart and Middelkoop 2011). Traditional dashboards were usually closed systems made for specific hardware or generic low resolution displays like televisions. Using web standards and protocols allows a more flexible design but poses some challenges. One of the challenges of moving from proprietary applications on specific hardware, or print media at fixed resolutions in general, is that modern webpages have to be designed for multiple screen layouts. The same data has to be available and usable from a widescreen desktop computer all the way down to a vertically oriented smartphone. In the past, this was dealt with by having separate sites for mobile devices and for desktops. These sites had different layouts, graphics, and fonts tailored for the resolution of the viewing device. This type of setup required the maintenance of multiple sets of code and webpages. This is no longer the case. Websites today use responsive design that adapts to the device it is displayed on.

Responsive design allows for flexibility of viewing devices. When a device requests a webpage it communicates to the web server certain information including the web browser and the size of the window the page will be displayed on called a viewport. Responsive design takes the size of the viewport and dynamically rearranges the page layout based on that size. This rearrangement usually means resizing text and graphics first. Resizing can only work to a limited point before the fonts and images become too small to read. At that point, the page will stack elements on a page so they are vertically aligned. This stacking occurs down the infinite scrolling space of the webpage. This design technique is associated with the devices that will consume content at smaller resolutions. Smaller screens are often touchscreens on smartphones. Unlike traditional mouse and keyboard setups, modern touch screens make it easy to flick the screen and quickly move vertically. Thus stacking information in a vertical layout using a larger font is a better configuration than forcing users to find scroll bars or pinch and zoom around a page. Another benefit to vertical stacking, especially in bandwidth limited mobile devices, is that off screen content can be loaded while the user interacts with the initial content. There is no apparent waiting for content to load, or frustrating rearrangement of the page as new content is added. Stacked content is backfilled in the few seconds the user begins to interact with the initial information.

Using web technologies to display content also allows researchers to take advantage of webpage interaction tracking software. This software can be used by websites to see which parts of their websites draw more attention or where visitors are coming from when they arrive at a webpage. On commercial websites, they are used to convert clicks to sales but they can also be used by researchers to evaluate interactions with a research instrument. In the case of the EIS, there are several metrics that can be collected. The tracking software shows where users are clicking or touching. It also shows where they are visiting the website from and what types of devices they are using.

Navigation between the pages of the EIS was another aspect that had to be taken into account with the design of the EIS. Navigation was affected by two aspects of the EIS; security and the touch control interface. The EIS is mounted in a public area where anyone can interact with it. There is a risk that users will try to navigate outside the EIS website area. To prevent this, the EIS is displayed in kiosk mode without the URL bar or the normal control buttons. This prevents users from going outside of the EIS but also limits the navigation options to the links provided. This limited navigation has to allow the user to get back to any place they navigated to without the use of the back button. This navigation limitation also limits linking to outside websites. One of the advantages of using webpages is the ability to link out to authoritative data and references. This is particularly salient for academic researchers who want to cite literature and data sources. In the case of the EIS, information about conversion rates, links to academic articles, and sources of information about conservation are all viable links.

One method for coping with these limitations is using modal windows. Modals are overlay windows similar to popups but have much more functionality. Unlike popups, they are part of the actual page, they are just not viewable until the user activates them. As they are part of the page, they do not suffer from being blocked like popups. Common uses for modals include light boxes that show pictures in full size so the page only has to initially load a smaller thumbnail or embedding PDFs. In situations like the EIS when there is limited navigation control, and the design prefers to keep the information in the initial screen view, there are two key utilizations of modals. The first use is allowing a designer to display additional information while still having the original page in the background, easily accessible by closing the modal box. In the case of the EIS they are used for the context tables that put the energy use in context of other electricity uses (see Figure 13.2). These modal windows display additional information without navigating off the page without a back button. The second use is loading outside webpages within the modal windows. This provides access to external resources but controls where the user can go. It also maintains programmatic control of the webpage in case there are background processes like an inactivity timeout monitor that resets the page when a user walks away.

13.3   Examination of Use

In initial prototypes using standard displays the thinking was "the bigger the better." More signage real estate allowed the display of more information and could be seen further away. However, when interacting with the EIS using touch, this thinking was quickly refuted. Touch was an important aspect because it simplified interaction with the dashboard. A user can directly interact with the system without having to use a keyboard and mouse. From an installation standpoint, a touch interface makes installation easier because a mouse and keyboard don't have to be mounted. Mounting hardware using input devices is more complicated and expensive. It can limit the areas where the signage can be installed. It usually requires more robust mounting and may take more space in areas like entrances where space is at a premium and may be influenced by building and fire codes.

Another characteristic of touch is that it may limit the size of the display. Large screens may be viewable from longer distances and allow the display of more information but interacting with them through touch is awkward. The user is tethered to the interface by the length of their arm and the bigger the interface the more the user has to swing their head around to see the information. Many "smart board" systems used in classrooms have touch capabilities but also have remote units that allow a teacher to interact from a distance so they are seeing the display as the students do. Large displays may look good in movies but from a practical use perspective they pose challenges to designers who want users to interact with information being displayed.

Early tests with the initial prototype revealed an oversight of design regarding the touch interface. One of the design issues that involved touch was communication to the observer that the sign is in fact a touch screen. Digital signage is becoming more common. As hardware becomes cheaper, digital signage is augmenting traditional signage for wayfinding, menu boards, and other information display. However, all of this signage is not touch interactive. Observations by the EIS designers revealed that many signs are not clear whether they are touch interactive. Afraid of damaging the equipment, users timidly poke the sign in the corner to see if there is any interaction.

13.4   Informed Redesign

After observing this uncertain interaction, the EIS was designed with an explicit invitation to interact with touch by using a small ribbon in the upper left hand corner. As most users will look across media from upper left to right they will see this ribbon first. This ribbon though is not necessary if the EIS is being viewed through a device other than the signage installed in the study building. Users from the web will know the capabilities of their devices. For this reason, the display of this ribbon is controlled with a cookie. A cookie is a small file that websites use to remember visitors and persist interactions over time. By default, the EIS does not display the touch banner. However, if the client identifies itself as a signage machine using a cookie set by visiting an unpublished page on the site, code in the website inserts the banner on the webpage to make it explicit to the viewer that the signage is a touch unit.

Touch also impacts a physical installation because units that support touch are much more expensive. For the EIS installation, 27-inch units were used that cost around $500 each. At the time of writing, 50-inch non-touch displays can be purchased for much less than this. The designers contemplated using a hybrid system of interactive and larger read only units. It was determined that the building placed limitations on where signage could be reasonable displayed and a system of smaller touch only systems was used.

An additional redesign step was to lockdown the EIS signage so that they were harder to tamper with. Initially, the EIS was put into a limited kiosk mode and password protected but the system was tampered with. Several times the displays were found not showing the EIS or with a web browser open and a webpage that was not the EIS being displayed. One of the lessons learned about public installations is that designers must take into account the relationship between features and security. The more features are exposed to the user, the greater the likelihood that the user can operate the installation in an unintended way. The designers imposed stricter security on the signage kiosks.

One final redesign involved the tracking software that collects user interaction with the website. Using modals poses challenges when trying to capture data about interaction with the EIS. This is because modals link internally within a page instead of to another page. Many web interaction tracking tools such as Google Analytics use clicks on links to additional pages to measure interaction with a website. Google Analytics can provide a large amount of tracking data with very little configuration so it can be implemented by novice programmers. Google Analytics allows tracking of many types of events but tracking modals requires additional coding to work. There are other packages available that capture heatmaps of clicks on webpages. These heatmaps can provide useful data visualization but they are of limited use for analytics. They rely on a Euclidean grid to describe where users clicked and cannot easily be aggregated to button clicks.

13.5   Lessons for Future Development

The use of touch had an inordinately large impact on the design of the EIS. It allowed a simplified design that focused on presenting the information without a lot of busy chrome. It also allowed easy navigation around the EIS. At the same time it limited the size of the units that could be comfortably used with touch interaction. The responsive design employed in the display of the dashboard facilitated a flexible layout that could accommodate being displayed on many different sized devices. It takes advantage of the best parts of the limited, touch-enabled display real estate of mobile devices while expanding to full size on larger displays.

References

Bendoly, Elliot. 2016. "Fit, bias and enacted sensemaking in data visualization: frameworks for continuous development in operations and supply chain management analytics." *Journal of Business Logistics* 37(1), 6–17.

Capehart, Barney L., and Timothy Middelkoop. 2011. *Handbook of web-based energy information and control systems*. Lilburn, GA: Fairmont Press.

Ehrhardt-Martinez, Karen, Kat A. Donnelly, and Skip Laitner. 2010. A*dvanced metering initiatives and residential feedback programs: a meta-review for household electricity-saving opportunities*. American Council for an Energy-Efficient Economy, Washington, DC.

EIA. 2015a. "How much coal, natural gas, or petrolium is used to generate a kilowatthour of electricty?" www.eia.gov/tools/faqs/faq.cfm?id=667&t=2 [accessed January 27, 2016].

EIA. 2015b. "How much energy is consumed in residential and commercial buildings in the United States? - FAQ – US Energy Information Administration (EIA)." www.eia. gov/tools/faqs/faq.cfm?id=86&t=1 [accessed January 27, 2016].

Gulbinas, Rimas, Rishee K. Jain, and John E. Taylor. 2014. "BizWatts: A modular socio-technical energy management system for empowering commercial building occupants to conserve energy." *Applied Energy* 136, 1076–1084. doi: 10.1016/j.apenergy.2014.07.034.

Lehrer, David, and Janani Vasudev. 2011. Visualizing Energy Information in Commercial Buildings: A Study of Tools, Expert Users, and Building Occupants.

Petersen, John E., Vladislav Shunturov, Kathryn Janda, Gavin Platt, and Kate Weinberger. 2007. "Dormitory residents reduce electricity consumption when exposed to real-time visual feedback and incentives." *International Journal of Sustainability in Higher Education* 8(1), 16–33.

Sovacool, Benjamin. 2009. "The cultural barriers to renewable energy and energy efficiency in the United States." *Technology in Society* 31(4), 365–373. doi: 10.1016/j.techsoc. 2009.10.009.

Troy, Austin. 2012. *The very hungry city: urban energy efficiency and the economic fate of cities.* New Haven, CT: Yale University Press.

INDEX

Taylor & Francis eBooks

Helping you to choose the right eBooks for your Library

Add Routledge titles to your library's digital collection today. Taylor and Francis ebooks contains over 50,000 titles in the Humanities, Social Sciences, Behavioural Sciences, Built Environment and Law.

Choose from a range of subject packages or create your own!

Benefits for you

>> Free MARC records
>> COUNTER-compliant usage statistics
>> Flexible purchase and pricing options
>> All titles DRM-free.

Benefits for your user

>> Off-site, anytime access via Athens or referring URL
>> Print or copy pages or chapters
>> Full content search
>> Bookmark, highlight and annotate text
>> Access to thousands of pages of quality research at the click of a button.

| REQUEST YOUR **FREE** INSTITUTIONAL TRIAL TODAY | **Free Trials Available** We offer free trials to qualifying academic, corporate and government customers. |

eCollections – Choose from over 30 subject eCollections, including:

Archaeology	Language Learning
Architecture	Law
Asian Studies	Literature
Business & Management	Media & Communication
Classical Studies	Middle East Studies
Construction	Music
Creative & Media Arts	Philosophy
Criminology & Criminal Justice	Planning
Economics	Politics
Education	Psychology & Mental Health
Energy	Religion
Engineering	Security
English Language & Linguistics	Social Work
Environment & Sustainability	Sociology
Geography	Sport
Health Studies	Theatre & Performance
History	Tourism, Hospitality & Events

For more information, pricing enquiries or to order a free trial, please contact your local sales team: **www.tandfebooks.com/page/sales**

 Routledge Taylor & Francis Group | The home of Routledge books | **www.tandfebooks.com**